Here's what people are saying a

An Insider's Guide to Managing Life

“Got Parts is a very well conceived and useful tool, partic ID from a more functional perspective. I believe the straigh s of "things to do" in an individual's treatment of DID this p in making this treatment more effective, informed and efficient. Since I believe much, if not most, of DID treatment progress happens outside of the therapeutic hour, this guidebook is the perfect companion for a DID patient.” —Peter A. Maves, Ph.D., ISSD Fellow

“Got Parts is an excellent book: it is wonderfully clear, concise and compassionate. I have worked full time with MPD clients for 15 years and this book would be the first required reading. Having a resource book such as this would have made my client's lives much easier. I will require it for any new clients, refer it to other therapists who do this work, and have even recommended it for clients who are much farther along in their healing. It is a definite keeper and I would recommend that you let the ISSD know about it when you have it published.” —Karen Hutchins, MA LPC

“Got Parts is an excellent resource for helping people bring order out of internal chaos. It is reassuring, clear, direct, and hopeful. A great tool for working therapeutically with one’s internal family.” —Patricia Sherman, LCSW

“Got Parts represents a systematic, structured program geared towards positive results for those labeled DID. Its focus on individual responsibility is refreshing in this day and age of blame shifting and excuse making! This is a must read regardless of one's support of or opposition to the medical model.”

—James Walter Clifton, MS, Ph.D. LCSW, LMHC

"DID is a heatedly-contested mental health diagnosis and it is entangled with no less controversial issues such as false memories. The author of this book avoids these pitfalls by concentrating on the victims. In an unusually empathic and straightforward tome, she successfully tackles the subjective experience of having DID: how does it feel? How to cope with it? What to avoid? The book is firmly grounded in state of the art knowledge about this disorder—but combines it with useful lists of do's and don'ts derived from the combined experience of numerous sufferers.
Recommended."

—Sam Vaknin, Ph.D. Author of "Malignant Self Love - Narcissism Revisited"

"I strongly recommend this book as an easily read, straightforward and insightful recovery tool for my clients with DID. It is must read for any person who is struggling to come to terms with their DID as well as the people who love and/or support them."

— Ian Landry, MA MSW RSW, Nova Scotia, Canada

New Horizons in Therapy Series:

- *Got parts? A Survivor's Guide to Managing Life Successfully with Dissociative Identity Disorder)*

Series Editor: Robert Rich, Ph.D.

"To be what we are,
and to become what we are capable of becoming,
is the only end in life"

—Robert Louis Stevenson (June 1880)

Loving Healing Press is dedicated to producing books about innovative and rapid therapies which redefine what is possible for healing the mind and spirit.

Loving Healing Press

got parts?

An INSIDER'S GUIDE to MANAGING LIFE SUCCESSFULLY with DISSOCIATIVE IDENTITY DISORDER

by ATW

Loving Healing Press

Got parts? : an insider's guide to managing life successfully with dissociative identity disorder

First Edition: January 2005
ISBN-10: 1932690042

Publisher's Cataloging-in-Publication Data

W., A.T.
Got parts? : an insider's guide to managing life successfully with dissociative identity disorder / by A.T.W.
p. cm.
Includes bibliographical references and index.
ISBN-10 1-932690-03-4

1. Multiple personality. 2. Post-traumatic stress disorder. 3. Life Change events--Psychological aspects. 4. Incest--Psychological aspects. 5. Adult child sexual abuse victims--rehabilitation. I. Title.

RC569.5 .M8 2005
616.85236 -- dc22 2004096989

Distributed by:
Baker & Taylor

Published by:
Loving Healing Press
5145 Pontiac Trail
Ann Arbor, MI 48105
USA

http://www.LovingHealing.com or
info@LovingHealing.com
Fax +1 734 663 6861

Loving Healing Press

Loving Healing Press

~~ Dedication ~~

This book is dedicated to all those whose suffering though trauma and wounding has resulted in fragmenting of self into separate selves... 'multiple personalities'.

It is our hope that the ideas contained within these pages will help you to feel courage and hope, and to come to find ways of managing your diagnosis, and the circumstances of your life—and to heal, rebuild and reclaim your life.

~~ Disclaimer ~~

The ideas, concepts, phrasing, wordings, and lay-definitions contained in this book are ones used by myself, my System, my therapist, and various persons from my DID groups, past and present.

This work is not intended to be a scholarly compendium, but is, rather, a lay-accounting of what has been helpful on our personal path of trauma recovery, and re-integration of alter personalities.

Information in this book is neither intended to supersede medical advice, nor to replace professional counsel by a qualified mental-health clinician or therapist.

About our Series Editor, Robert Rich, Ph.D.

Loving Healing Press is pleased to announce Robert Rich, Ph.D. as Series Editor for the *New Horizons in Therapy Series*. This exciting new series plans to bring you the best of person-centered therapies in practical application, theory, and self-help formats.

Robert Rich, M.Sc., Ph.D., M.A.P.S., A.A.S.H. is a highly experienced counseling psychologist. His web site www.anxietyanddepression-help.com is a storehouse of helpful information for people suffering from almost any way we can make ourselves and each other unhappy.

Bob is also a multiple award-winning writer of both fiction and non-fiction, and a professional editor. His writing is displayed at www.bobswriting.com. You are advised not to visit him there unless you have the time to get lost for a while.

Two of his books are tools for psychological self-help: *Anger and Anxiety: Be in Charge of your Emotions and Control Phobias* and *Personally Speaking: Single Session Email Therapy with Dr Bob Rich*. However, his philosophy and psychological knowledge come through in all his writing, which is perhaps why three of his books have won international awards, and he has won many minor prizes. Dr. Rich currently resides in Wombat Hollow in Australia.

~~ Acknowledgements ~~

Over the years, there were many folks who befriended us, and whose support, guidance, expertise, insights, and experiences were instrumental in enabling us to get to where we are today—guess maybe you could say that sometimes it takes a village to help a System. In this attempt to give acknowledgement, if we have missed anyone, we humbly apologize. Please know your name is written in our heart.

Thanks go to John A. Newberg, M.Div., who went above and beyond the call to travel with us to the end of the beginning; and to Richard F. (Rick) Ritter, MSW, and Laurie Rainey Schmidt, MS—our wingmen, (and sometime tag-team of Bad Cop/Good Cop). There are no words adequate to our depth of feeling for you.

With her wisdom, her quiet, fearless spirit, generosity, compassionate patience, and willingness to learn with us along the way, Laurie has become treasured and invaluable friend, teacher, spiritual guide, and role model.

Rick Ritter's counseling-consulting practice, Stress Operations Group, Inc., was where we were first diagnosed with multiple personalities. Rick's skill in working with trauma survivors of all sorts, and his unique model of re-integration of alter personalities have been the cornerstone of our healing work. The ideas in *got parts?* are a compilation of Rick's, and of the many DID clients he has worked with over the last twenty-five years. The result is an amalgam so homogenous and smooth, that it is difficult to know exactly what idea came from whom...

and in this spirit, thanks go also to those persons from our DID groups—past and present—who walk beside us, leaving courageous footprints for others to follow. You have raged with us, cried with us, laughed with us, inspired us, pushed us beyond what we believed were our limits, sat in the silence with us, listened compassionately and tirelessly, and offered equally your ideas, your own stories of pain and healing, and your friendship. We have learned so much from all of you... including from some who have lived the hard truths that come from choosing to not do the work.

Thanks go to Allison, John, Jan, Leigh, Suzie, Kim, Amanda, Jan, Jo, A., Laura, Angie, Elizabeth, Mike, Kim, Rebecca, Bobbie, Kathy, Genny, Rebecca, Rita, Katie, D., Kristine, Tammy, Gina, Josh, Leanne...

You may never know the long-range impact-for-good of your life on others whom you may never meet.

Thanks go to Patrick and Janet, for caring about our safety and supporting us, and to Phyllis, Sunny, and James, who helped to facilitate our leaving our desperate situation.

Gratitude is also extended to Shirley and Tina (among others) of the YWCA Women's Shelter Self-Sufficiency Program for the initial safe place to live when we got out, and for all we learned there.

In spite of a number of folks along the way, some of them folks in the medical and mental health community, some in agencies and in bureaucratic positions, others whom we thought were our friends...who, by way of their own fears, prejudices, and carefully guarded ignorance, and their own wounded and un-healed psyches, impeded, even sabotaged our getting help and our progress...

...there were others who behaved decently, compassionately, generously.

Thanks go to the many kind souls we have met along the way, who have made the way a little less lonely, a little less dark. Heather, Renee, Helen-Clare, Tom, Nathan, Fritz, Nancy, Tanya, Jenny, Laura, Amanda, and Judy, are only a few... I hope you know who you are.

We extend heart-felt gratitude and appreciation to Pastors Jeremy Ashworth and Steve Clapp, and to the Truthseekers Class and the rest of the Lincolnshire community for their affirmation, support, compassion, and belief in us.

Thanks go from the bottom of our heart to Victor R. Volkman of Loving Healing Press, who saw something unique shine in the manuscript, who believed in its potential to help a wider group of wounded folks, and who was willing to facilitate that vision become reality through the publication of *got parts?* Thank you, thank you, thank you.

And finally, warm, loving thanks, and a grateful spirit, go to Beth Lee Cripe, ... our truest kindred spirit, who never gave up on us through the long haul... and who in return, got more friends than she ever dreamed of...

We would not be here, in this place, without all of you. Thank you.

~~Table of Contents

~~Foreword by Rick Ritter, MSW ~~

The creation of this book has been a process—a process much like working with persons with dissociative disorders (Dissociative Identity Disorder specifically).

I would liken the process to the building and development of an organic garden. Building and tending to the soil leads to fruition in the vegetables and fruit products that the soil produces over time and... produces continuously as the gardener replenishes the soil in one way or another so that the garden will continue to produce without depleting or harming the soil. Just as the garden requires preventative maintenance, likewise so does the internal community of the dissociative person.

After a number of years of clients being dissatisfied with the materials available to them that would talk to them on their level in their language and support their internal growth came the inspiration to write *got parts?*

Got parts? is a work from the heart and because it is from the heart and experience of dissociative persons I believe that it will speak to them, regardless of where they are in their healing journey, in ways that other writings haven't.

I have had the privilege of working alongside the author as they have struggled against the odds and against the attitudes of many people in their life to come to this point in their journey. The author has humbly worked on and worked through many obstacles to bring you, the reader, this gift from their heart.

From the earliest lines and the trepidation that arose at so many varied points along the way I believe the writings will become a significant piece of the rebuilding of one's foundation if they are dissociative, and if they are a friend or family member it will bring them closer to understanding what others live and struggle with daily.

These writings are but a stone in a new foundation one can lay for themselves and their lives. There is no magic dust; there is no potion, only hard persistent work with supportive people and tools in your hands to forge a brand new way of living.

One of the outcomes we hope for in these writings is that they assist you in being able to, in a sense, see through the pain—understanding hopefully that there is a space beyond this work where all isn't so gloomy. It is beneficial to be able to be comforted by others who have been through this healing process and know that they were assisted by some or all of the helpful words and hints contained herein.

It is our wish that in reading, working, and processing this information that you will feel embraced, comforted and strengthened in the end.

Peace to you all as you continue on your journey.

~~Preface: What is Dissociative Identity Disorder (DID)?~~

Reprinted with permission from the Sidran Institute

Dissociative Disorders

Recently considered rare and mysterious psychiatric curiosities, Dissociative Identity Disorder (DID) (previously known as Multiple Personality Disorder—MPD) and other Dissociative Disorders are now understood to be fairly common effects of severe trauma in early childhood. Most typical cause is extreme, repeated physical, sexual, and/or emotional abuse.

In the Diagnostic and Statistical Manual of Mental Disorders-IV (American Psychiatric Association, 1994), Multiple Personality Disorder (MPD) was changed to Dissociative Identity Disorder (DID), reflecting changes in professional understanding of the disorder resulting from significant empirical research.

Posttraumatic Stress Disorder (PTSD), widely accepted as a major mental illness affecting 8% of the general population in the United States, is closely related to Dissociative Disorders. In fact, 80-100% of people diagnosed with a Dissociative Disorder also have a secondary diagnosis of PTSD. The personal and societal cost of trauma disorders is extremely high. Recent research suggests the risk of suicide attempts among people with trauma disorders may be even higher than among people who have major depression. In addition, there is evidence that people with trauma disorders have higher rates of alcoholism, chronic medical illnesses, and abusiveness in succeeding generations.

What is dissociation?

Dissociation is a mental process that produces a lack of connection in a person's thoughts, memories, feelings, actions, or sense of identity. During the period of time when a person is dissociating, certain information is not associated with other information as it normally would be. For example, during a traumatic experience, a person may dissociate the memory of the place and circumstances of the trauma from his ongoing memory, resulting in a temporary mental escape from the fear and pain of the trauma and, in some cases, a memory gap surrounding the experience. Because this process can produce changes in memory, people who frequently dissociate often find their senses of personal history and identity are affected.

Most clinicians believe that dissociation exists on a continuum of severity. This continuum reflects a wide range of experiences and/or symptoms. At one end are mild dissociative experiences common to most people, such as daydreaming, highway hypnosis, or ‘getting lost’ in a book or movie, all of which involve ‘losing touch’ with conscious awareness of one's immediate surroundings. At the other extreme is complex, chronic dissociation, such as in cases of Dissociative Disorders, which may result in serious impairment or inability to function. Some people with Dissociative Disorders can hold highly responsible jobs, contributing to society in a variety of professions, the arts, and public service—appearing to function normally to coworkers, neighbors, and others with whom they interact daily.

There is a great deal of overlap of symptoms and experiences among the various Dissociative Disorders, including DID. For the sake of clarity, this book will refer to Dissociative Disorders as a collective term. Individuals should seek help from qualified mental health providers to answer questions about their own particular circumstances and diagnoses.

How does a Dissociative Disorder develop?

When faced with overwhelmingly traumatic situations from which there is no physical escape, a child may resort to 'going away' in his or her head. Children typically use this ability as an extremely effective defense against acute physical and emotional pain, or anxious anticipation of that pain. By this dissociative process, thoughts, feelings, memories, and perceptions of the traumatic experiences can be separated off psychologically, allowing the child to function as if the trauma had not occurred.

Dissociative Disorders are often referred to as a highly creative survival technique because they allow individuals enduring 'hopeless' circumstances to preserve some areas of healthy functioning. Over time, however, for a child who has been repeatedly physically and sexually assaulted, defensive dissociation becomes reinforced and conditioned. Because the dissociative escape is so effective, children who are very practiced at it may automatically use it whenever they feel threatened or anxious—even if the anxiety-producing situation is not extreme or abusive.

Often, even after the traumatic circumstances are long past, the left-over pattern of defensive dissociation remains. Chronic defensive dissociation may lead to serious dysfunction in work, social, and daily activities.

Repeated dissociation may result in a series of separate entities, or mental states, which may eventually take on identities of their own. These entities may become the internal 'personality states' of a DID system. Changing between these states of consciousness is often described as 'switching.'

What are the symptoms of a Dissociative Disorder?

People with Dissociative Disorders may experience any of the following: depression, mood swings, suicidal tendencies, sleep disorders (insomnia, night terrors, and sleep walking), panic attacks and phobias (flashbacks, reactions to stimuli or 'triggers'), alcohol and drug abuse, compulsions and rituals, psychotic-like symptoms (including auditory and visual hallucinations), and eating disorders. In addition, individuals with Dissociative Disorders can experience headaches, amnesias, time loss, trances, and 'out of body experiences'. Some people with Dissociative Disorders have a tendency toward self-persecution, self-sabotage, and even violence (both self-inflicted and outwardly directed).

Who gets Dissociative Disorders?

The vast majority (as many as 98 to 99%) of individuals who develop Dissociative Disorders have documented histories of repetitive, overwhelming, and often life-threatening trauma at a sensitive developmental stage of childhood (usually before the age of nine), and they may possess an inherited biological predisposition for dissociation. In our culture the most frequent precursor to Dissociative Disorders is extreme physical, emotional, and sexual abuse in childhood, but survivors of other kinds of trauma in childhood (such as natural disasters, invasive medical procedures, war, kidnapping, and torture) have also reacted by developing Dissociative Disorders.

Current research shows that DID may affect 1% of the general population and perhaps as many as 5-20% of people in psychiatric hospitals, many of whom have received other diagnoses. The incidence rates are even higher among sexual-abuse survivors and individuals with chemical dependencies. These statistics put Dissociative Disorders in the same category as schizophrenia, depression, and anxiety, as one of the four major mental health problems today.

Most current literature shows that Dissociative Disorders are recognized primarily among females. The latest research, however, indicates that the disorders may be equally prevalent (but less frequently diagnosed) among the male population. Men with Dissociative Disorders are most likely to be in treatment for other mental illnesses or drug and alcohol abuse, or they may be incarcerated.

Why are Dissociative Disorders often misdiagnosed?

Dissociative Disorders survivors often spend years living with misdiagnoses, consequently floundering within the mental health system. They change from therapist to therapist and from medication to medication, getting treatment for symptoms but making little or no actual progress. Research has documented that on average, people with Dissociative Disorders have spent seven years in the mental health system prior to accurate diagnosis. This is common, because the list of symptoms that cause a person with a Dissociative Disorder to seek treatment is very similar to those of many other psychiatric diagnoses. In fact, many people who are diagnosed with Dissociative Disorders also have secondary diagnoses of depression, anxiety, or panic disorders.

Do people actually have 'Multiple Personalities'?

Yes, and no. One of the reasons for the decision by the psychiatric community to change the disorder's name from Multiple Personality Disorder to Dissociative Identity Disorder is that 'multiple personalities' is somewhat of a misleading term. A person diagnosed with DID feels as if she has within her two or more entities, or personality states, each with its own independent way of relating, perceiving, thinking, and remembering about herself and her life. If two or more of these entities take control of the person's behavior at a given time, a diagnosis of DID can be made. These entities previously were often called 'personalities,' even though the term did not accurately reflect the common definition of the word as the total aspect of our psychological makeup. Other terms often used by therapists and survivors to describe these entities are: 'alternate personalities', 'alters', 'parts', 'states of consciousness', 'ego states', and 'identities'. It is important to keep in mind that although these alternate states may appear to be very different, they are all manifestations of a single person.

Can Dissociative Disorders be cured?

Yes. Dissociative Disorders are highly responsive to individual psychotherapy, or 'talk therapy', as well as to a range of other treatment modalities, including medications, hypnotherapy, and adjunctive therapies such as art or movement therapy. In fact, among comparably severe psychiatric disorders, Dissociative Disorders may be the condition that carries the best prognosis if proper treatment is undertaken and completed. The course of treatment is long-term, intensive, and invariably painful, as it generally involves remembering and reclaiming the dissociated traumatic experiences. Nevertheless, individuals with Dissociative Disorders have been successfully treated by therapists of all professional backgrounds working in a variety of settings.

Where can I get more information?

From the Sidran Institute. Here is their press release:

At Sidran, we help people understand, manage, and treat dissociative and traumatic stress conditions. We are a national nonprofit organization and one of the nation's leading providers of traumatic stress education, publications, and resources. Sidran is dedicated to supporting people with traumatic stress conditions, providing education and training on treating and managing traumatic stress, promoting trauma-related advocacy, and informing the public on issues related to traumatic stress. Sidran Institute Press, our publishing division, is a leading publisher of books about trauma and dissociation.

The Sidran Bookshelf is a Web-based and mail order supplier of books, audio and videotapes, and informational materials of particular interest to Dissociative Disorder survivors, their supportive family and friends, and their therapists.

Sidran Institute Press publishes the highly acclaimed *Multiple Personality Disorder from the Inside Out*, a collection of writings about living with MPD by 146 survivors and their significant others. Sidran also publishes books essential to the library of any therapist dealing with dissociation, most recently *Growing Beyond Survival: A Self-Help Toolkit for Managing Traumatic Stress*. This self-regulation and symptom self-management workbook is written to empower dissociative survivors to take control of and de-escalate their most distressing trauma-related symptoms.

Growing Beyond Survival and other dissociation-related titles are available through our toll-free order desk at 888-825-8249.

In addition, Sidran has compiled lists of Dissociative Disorders support and treatment resources, available by calling our resource specialists at 410-825-8888.

The Sidran Institute 200 E. Joppa Road, Suite 207 Towson, MD 21286 USA
Phone: 410-825-8888 Fax: 410-337-0747 www.sidran.org

1 got parts?

~~You are not alone~~

No, really. Literally.

Maybe you have always known (or suspected) this. Maybe this news is shocking, baffling, dismaying, even unbelievable to you. Despite what you might believe or may have been told about yourself, you are not just 'moody'. Nor are you crazy or defective or possessed. You have what is commonly called 'multiple personalities'.

What used to be called Multiple Personality Disorder (MPD) has now been reclassified in the DSM IV diagnostic manual as Dissociative Identity Disorder (DID). Multiple personalities arise from traumatic events, things which are so overwhelming to body, mind, emotion, and spirit, that in an attempt to cope with—to physically or emotionally survive the event—a separate personality state, also known as a part, or an *alter* or alter personality, emerges to survive what is happening. This is known as *splitting*. One way of understanding personality states might be to think of it this way: when you think of a person you know, you are actually relating to or interacting with a 'personality state'. Usually there is one personality state (think of it as the 'driver') per one physical body (think of this as the 'vehicle'). In the case of someone who is has multiple personalities—DID—the vehicle (body) has more than one 'driver'.

The entirety of alters (or parts) which co-exist inside one individual physical body is known as a *System*.

Going back and forth between first one alter being 'out front' or 'presenting' (interacting with the outside world), then another alter coming to the fore to be out, is known as *switching*.

There is no shame in being DID. Having multiple personalities does not reflect a weak or flawed character, rather, the opposite. It is a testimony to the strong, creative, courageous human spirit, and its psychic imperative to survive.

These other alters—parts—are every bit as real as you are. It is essential that you become aware of all the alters who are a part of you, that you get to know each other, and that you become able to trust each other. In order to function successfully it will be critical that you-all work together to heal and reclaim your life/lives, and work toward developing a shared goal or vision of where and how you see yourself functioning in the outside world.

Parts are never going to disappear or go away; they will always be there, and part of you. Individual parts will always remain separately individual, but the goal of *re-integration* is to become aware of each other and working so seamlessly and cooperatively together, with shared information and regarding switches, that you can live and function in the outside world with a minimum of distress, without others even knowing about your multiplicity unless you choose to disclose it.

With belief, time, and a lot of hard work, it is possible to live not just a survival-level functional existence, but a rich and satisfying life with multiple personalities co-existing within the same physical body.

But it's not easy.

That's the idea behind this book: to share information culled from others who are also DID and who have learned from hard experience what works, what doesn't; what it takes to manage this diagnosis and to recover from the trauma that caused the splitting in the first place; and what it takes to have a System of alters who are working toward ever-higher levels of re-integration and who, in doing so, are living a better life than they ever thought possible. So...

"Just Sit Right Back And You'll Hear A Tale... ♫
♫ of what has worked for others...."

~~Getting to Know You~~

Getting To Know You, Getting To Know All About You

It is essential to get to know each individual alter, and the System-as-a-whole.

Once you, or your therapist have encountered an alter for the first time, that is the time to begin the process of getting acquainted with that part.

There is often upset, fear, confusion, anxiety—many emotions which you or the other alter may be feeling. The newly discovered part may or may not know where they are, or that time—sometimes years—has passed since they split off, or since they have last been 'out', and that circumstances have changed.

Go slowly, gently, and respectfully as you are getting to know newly-discovered parts...try putting yourself in their shoes and imagine how they might be feeling.

It's important to create an atmosphere and an environment in which this newly discovered part can feel as safe and welcome as possible. It will be very important to brief them on the System—to have them meet and get to know everyone else inside, and to come to understand how life is now, and how it differs from how it was when they split off.

Some Systems find that having a notebook in which you-all can write, and in which you can write to each other, can help facilitate this slow process of getting to know who all is a part of your System, what the other parts are like, and begin to build foundations of trust.

In order to get to know who is in your System, each individual alter needs to complete a piece of paper in the form of a circle (or triangle) which contains the following information: their name, their age (it might be an age range, like age 4-7), and their traits, strengths and skills. (All parts must have a name. If they do not have a name, they need to choose one. If their name was given to them by a perpetrator and is too upsetting or if it has a negative association, they may wish to change their name—that is perfectly ok. Any name that is not negative or triggering is fine—it does not have to be a standard 'proper name' as they are commonly thought of.) On the back of the circle or triangle they need to write down what caused them to split off.

Having a circle or triangle completed is a pre-requisite to entering the Safe Space/Dome explained a little later on page 15.

Parts (alters) also each need to write their individual histories—their life stories—as much as they can remember. Even if clearly recognizable memories are lacking, with only 'pictures' in their head, or fragments of something recalled it's important to write these down. Alters should do this even if they do not fully understand them, (or sometimes even believe them initially). Parts can always come back and examine them later, and to clarify, and/or add to these pictures or memory fragments if they remember things later.

Remembering things or processing memories can be a charged, or frightening, or uncomfortable time. It can help to imagine yourself being a reporter. This can take pressure off of needing to remember 'all the details' or not wanting to 'be wrong about something', if you simply just write down whatever comes to you down on paper without editing it, censoring it, or passing judgment—for the time being—on either its content, or on whether it is 100% accurate in every way. Simply write it down and come back to it later, when things may make more sense, or as additional information comes to you (or another part provides helpful information based on their own memories or information).

Young parts can dictate their story for someone else to write down, or they can draw it with pictures.

System-as-a-whole information can be learned by completing the following two projects: a System Map and a Timeline.

These two projects are tools to provide graphics which can aid in getting a different kind of look at your overall System. You can then gain a different perspective on information you may or may not already know, and see connections that may help you to understand your System better.

The System Map is like an internal family tree, though it can be drawn out in whatever format, in whatever way is easy for the System to understand. It will contain and illustrate information such as who split off from whom and how you all relate to each other. As you become more aware of your System over time, your System Map may grow as you encounter newly discovered parts. It may also change over time as you come to have greater understanding of your System and how you all relate to and interrelate with each other. Some System Maps appear on the following pages:

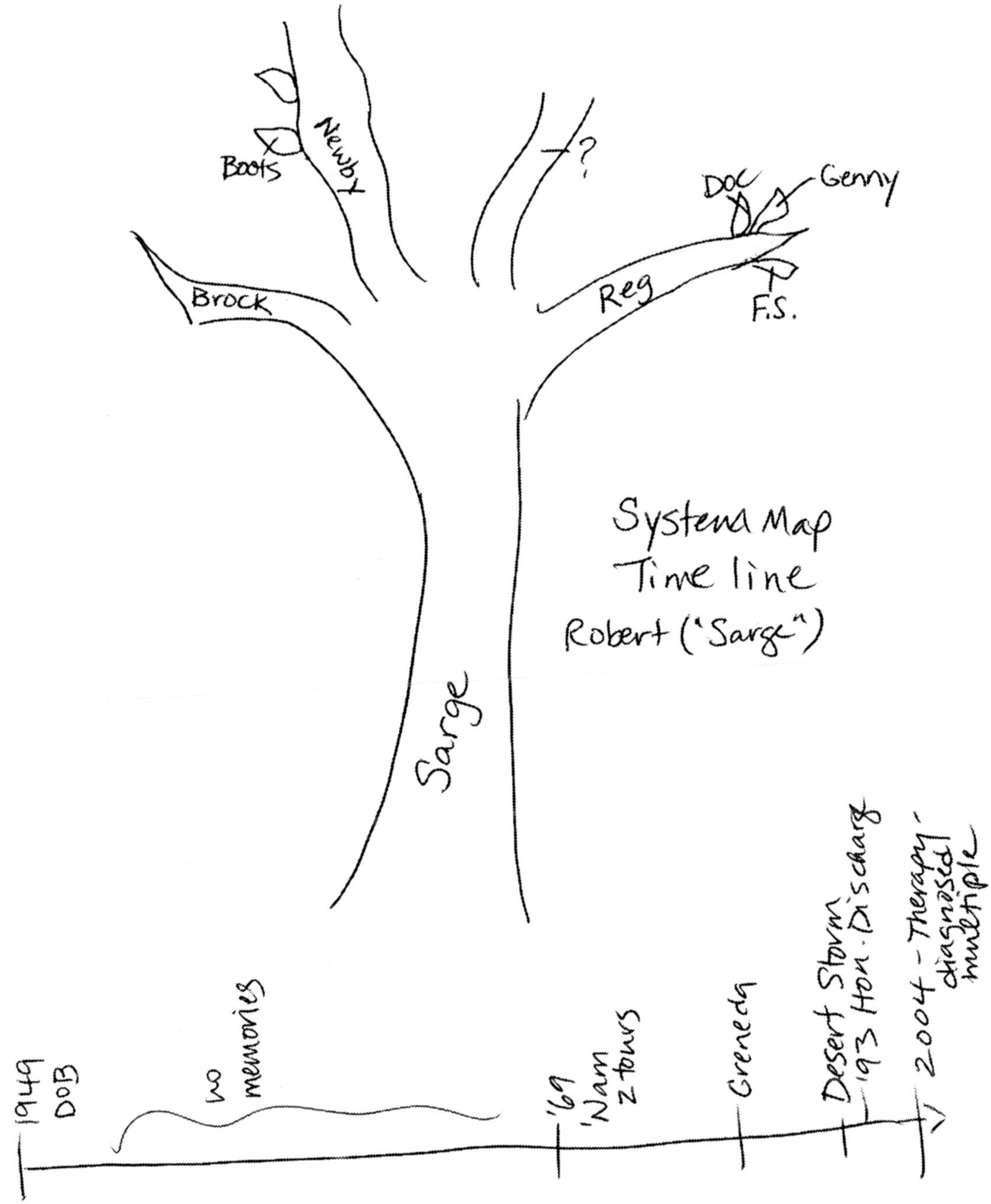

System Map (above) and Timeline (below) for Robert ("Sarge")

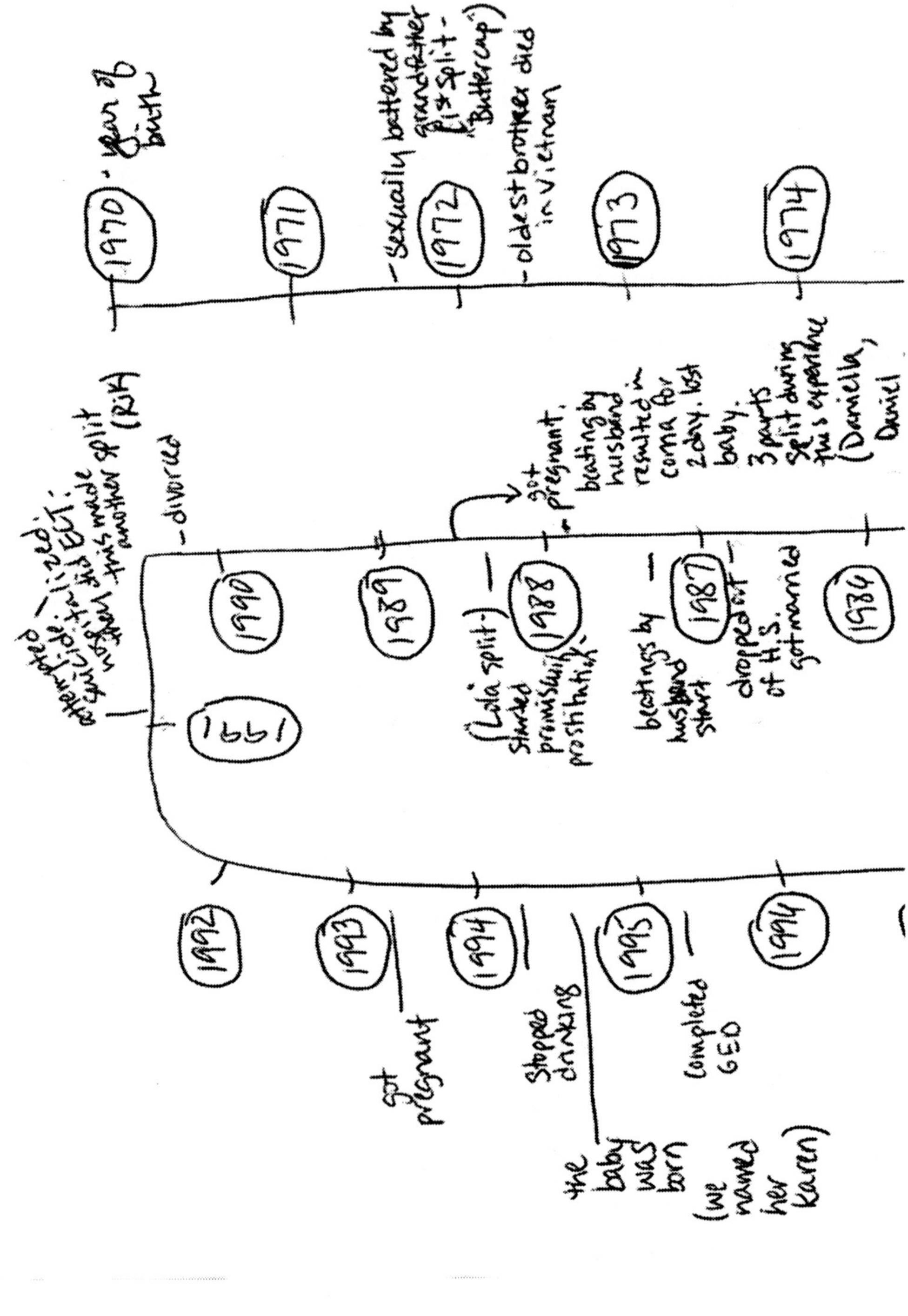
1970 · year of birth
1971
1972
- sexually battered by grandfather (1st split - "Buttercup")
- oldest brother died in Vietnam
1973
1974
1984
1987
1988
1989
1990
- divorced
1991
attempted suicide; hospitalized; they did ECT; this made another split (Rick)
got married
dropped out of H.S.
beatings by husband start
(Lola split) started promiscuity, prostitution
got pregnant, beating by husband resulted in coma for 2 days, lost baby, 3 parts split during this experience (Daniella, Daniel
1992
1993
1994
1995
1996
got pregnant
stopped drinking
completed GED
the baby was born (we named her Karen)

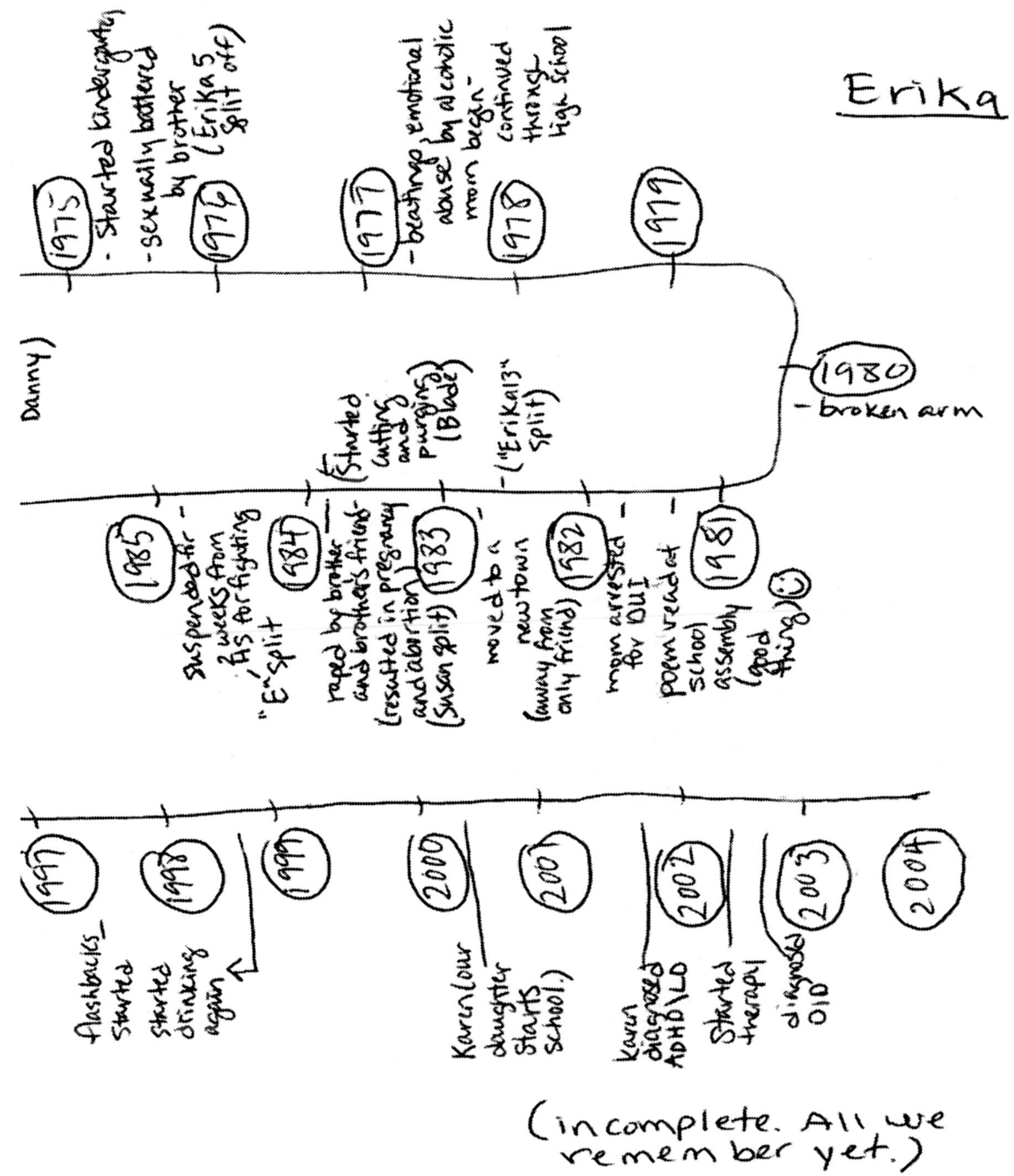
Erika
1975
- Started kindergarten
1976
- sexually battered by brother (Erika 5 split off)
1977
- beatings, emotional abuse by alcoholic mom begin - continued through high school
1978
1979
1980
- broken arm
1981
poem read at school assembly (good thing) :)
mom arrested for DUI
1982
moved to a new town (away from only friend)
- ("Erika13" split)
1983
raped by brother and brother's friends (resulted in pregnancy and abortion) (Susan split)
(Started cutting and purging) (Blade)
1984
1985
suspended for 2 weeks from HS for fighting
"E" split
Danny)
1997
flashbacks started
1998
started drinking again
1999
2000
Karen (our daughter starts school.)
2001
2002
Karen diagnosed ADHD/LD
Started therapy
2003
diagnosed DID
2004
(incomplete. All we remember yet.)

The Timeline is a straight line drawing accounting for the current age of the body, starting the year the body was born, marked off year by year, and continuing to the present year. Traumatic events and other important occurrences should be written down in the year they occurred, along with entries of who split off when. Just like the System Map, your Timeline may fill in more as you continue to do this work, continue to remember things, and continue to get to know your System, as some parts may have information that others in the System may not be aware of. Some timelines appear on the previous pages.

All of this information—the circles/triangles (see page 3) and life stories, and the System Map and the Timeline, need to be shared with everyone inside. All of this information needs to be shared with your therapist.

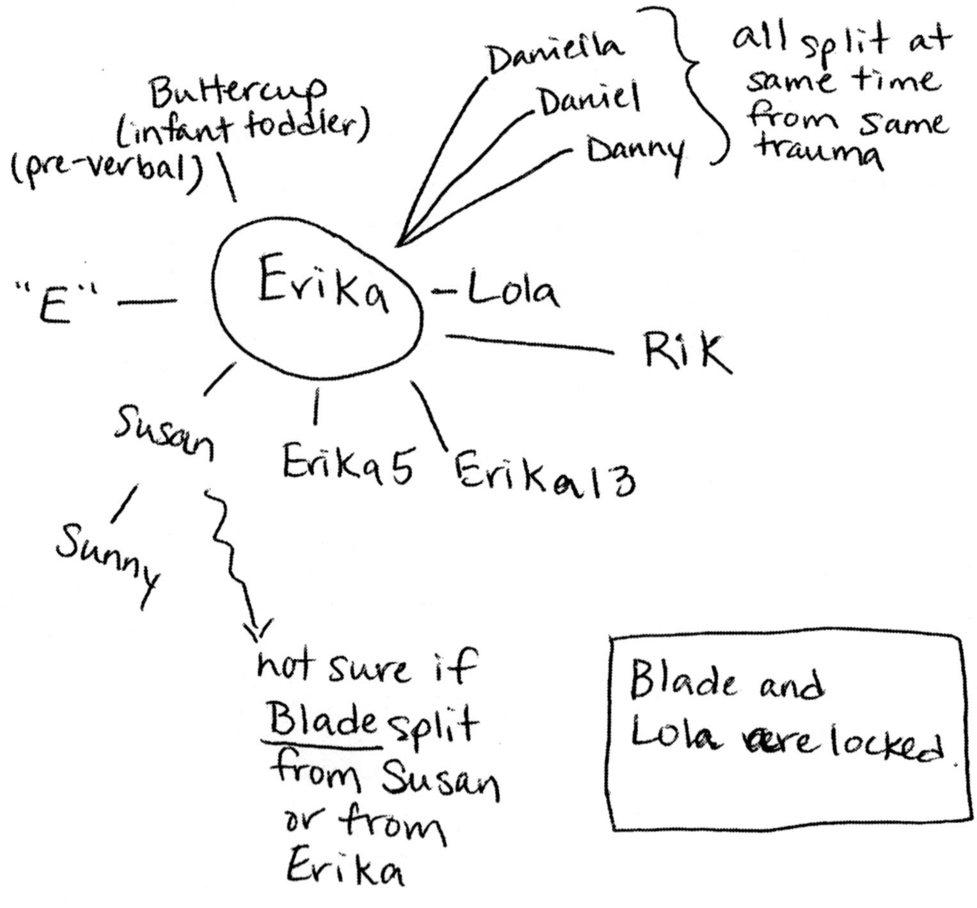

System Map for Erika

~~Respecting Each Other~~

♫ *"R-E-S-P-E-C-T: Find Out What It Means To (You-all)"* ♫

Every one of you exists for a reason.

When something perceived as traumatic or overwhelming occurs, and whoever is present (whoever is 'out', or 'there') isn't able to stay present and go through or take in that event or experience, either a new alter splits off, or another alter who is already a part of the System steps in to go through and 'hold' that trauma or distress, so you don't have to.

You actually owe other parts in your System your thanks—not your derision, contempt, or judgment.

The reverse is also true: what caused you to split off kept someone else inside from having to go through what you did. They owe you some appreciation.

It is very important to develop an attitude of gratitude for each other, and to show mutual respect.

A parallel aspect to the idea of mutual respect is this: because other selves (alter personalities/parts) also share residence in the same physical body that you do, your choices and behaviors affect everyone else inside. For example, a part who is bulimic may be inducing vomiting several times a day, and not personally 'mind' doing this and not think there is anything wrong with doing this. However there may be a four-year-old part who is confused and terrified, and hates that <u>her</u> throat is always raw from the continually forced vomiting.

The bulimic part's behavior is not just disrespectful, but actually abusive to others in the System. It is, of course, also disrespectful and abusive to (self) as an individual part. This is an example of an area in which contracts, discussed later on page 27, can prove invaluable.

~~Celebrate Diversity in your System~~

♫ *"We Are Family (I Got All My Parts within Me)"* ♫

Systems can have any number of alter personalities, from two to a great many. Generally, it is believed that the earlier the trauma occurs, the more extreme the trauma is, and the longer time during which it occurs directly bear upon the number of resulting parts. The kind and amount of support one receives at the time of the trauma, as well as afterward, can also make a difference.

Alter personalities can be almost as different as you can imagine.

There can be parts of any age—young parts, old parts, parts the actual age of the physical body. Some parts claim an age older than the actual age of the physical body. There can be male parts present in a female body or female parts present in a male body.

There can be parts who are conservative while others are flamboyant.

There can be bookworms while others have no interest in reading; parts who are athletic while others are not similarly skilled; parts with parenting skills while others do not relate well to children; parts who might be sexual doyennes or sirens while others do not enjoy or cannot tolerate sexual contact; or parts who are gay, lesbian, or bisexual when the rest of the System is heterosexual.

There may be parts who hold deep spiritual beliefs while others are agnostic. There may be parts who are dyslexic or have other learning disabilities, or who are functionally deaf or blind. There may be parts who speak with a brogue, twang, drawl, or other accent; there may be a part who stutters or lisps. Some parts may even speak a foreign language the others do not know.

Not all of these may be present in any one System, or in your particular System, as all Systems are different. Still, finding diverse parts in one's System can be unnerving and hard to comprehend and adjust to until you-all become aware of who is in your System, get to know each other, and appreciate the diversity in your System.

It is important to eventually come to the understanding that whoever is in your System, <u>every</u> alter brings unique skills, strengths, knowledge, experiences and insights to the System-as-a-whole. This affords a wider base from which to act, which benefits everyone.

There is a reason why each of you exists, and without all of you—everyone in the System—the mind and the body might not have survived what you went through, and what you experienced.

Everyone has something of value to contribute to the System. Everyone who is interested in getting better is vital to the healthy functioning of the System.

Believe it or not, alters (parts) are assets, not liabilities.

~~Parts and the Roles they Play~~

Sometimes parts split off, or are created, not necessarily because of a particular abuse or trauma, but because of a stressful situation that was deemed threatening. Necessity may dictate that parts assume certain roles or duties in order to get by, or 'stay safe', or to not attract unwanted attention.

An example is a part who can focus enough to go to school; or who is better able to fulfill the role as parent than others in the System; one who handles conflict better, or who is more poised in social situations, or on the job; or who can be intimate with a spouse or partner if the System is in a marriage or committed relationship. These parts may or may not have suffered a primary trauma.

Some Systems—though not all—find that there is a part who functions as a kind of 'Historian' or 'Watcher' or 'Librarian'—they are known by different names in different Systems. This part often has knowledge or memories, or knows things that other parts may not. It may be the part to know about past trauma.

Though not found in every System, it is not uncommon to find parts who might have what might be termed 'archetype' roles—'Inner Healer', 'Wise One', and 'Protector' are a few examples, though Systems may call them by different names.

Sometimes the role of Protector can have a flip side to it. Some Systems have found that their 'protector' tries to protect individual parts and the System with outmoded or mistaken ideas of what safety really is.

Sometimes they attempt to 'protect' themselves or the System by being obnoxious, aloof, or overly and inappropriately aggressive in order to drive others away, or keep others from getting to know them or the System better. Sometimes they bully, even abuse other parts—sometimes to the point of self-violence or self-mutilation—in order to keep parts quiet so they don't tell about abuses they have suffered and do their best to insure that parts keep numb so secrets remain secret. If your System has a part or parts who engages in these, or similar behaviors—whether in the name of being a 'protector' or not—it will be crucial to identify these parts, and essential that they begin to work with your therapist to create healthier, more functional ways of staying safe that are more appropriate to current situations. They could also be encouraged to take on a new and different role, perhaps.

So here is a question—can a part also be a perpetrator?

This is a thorny question. In some respects, a part can be a perpetrator, if they are abusing or perpetrating violence on someone—including others in the System—

or if they behave in a menacing, threatening, or controlling way that prevents another from their own choices and freedoms and personal safety, including both other alters in the System as well as outside persons.

How does this shake out in response to others (outside or inside)? Chances are very high there will be a lot of chaos and confusion and life will be convoluted and ripe with contradictions, smallness, negativity, and lacking peace and order. This is a serious issue that needs to be addressed with your therapist. The part may need to be in 'lockdown' (explained in detail on page 24) until the seriousness can be properly assessed and dealt with.

Sometimes roles become so rigid and compartmentalized that the rest of the System comes to believe that a given part is the only part who is able to (or who is allowed to) take on that particular task or job in the System. Although highly defined and static roles may have been a necessary coping/survival strategy in the past, it can sometimes hinder or cripple a System from being able to move into healthier and more functional patterns of living today.

It is important for the System-as-a-whole, for individual parts to learn other tasks, and to eventually share (or at least have the capability to share) roles and responsibilities—though obviously with advance planning and foresight and discretion.

This enables parts to take 'breathers' and breaks from something they have been doing for perhaps a very long time. Parts may be tired of, even resent always having to be the one responsible for what may be tedious, difficult or unpleasant. Sharing is also a good idea in case there is a reason the regular part is not able to take on and do her normal tasks.

Once there may have been a need for rigid roles; now this need may no longer exist, or it may not be as necessary or urgent (but see page 39).

Sharing roles, responsibilities or tasks also enables other parts to help the System's successful functioning in the outside world. Then, these parts can grow and mature individually. It also gives the System the opportunity to feel first-hand appreciation for what parts have done and contributed to the System's survival and success, as well as better understanding of what it takes to keep the System functioning well today.

~~Inside Kids~~

♫ *"Here's the story of a lovely System,* ♫
who was bringing up some very lovely kids..."

Now, about the 'inside kids'...

If your System has young parts, and that is not uncommon if abuse or other trauma happened at an early age, they need to be afforded the same consideration and respect as any other alter. And, just like 'outside' kids, whether they are toddlers or young children or teenagers, they cannot be allowed to run wild and unsupervised doing whatever they want whenever they want. They need manners, rules, guidance and boundaries. They also need love and inclusion, as well as clear, correct, age-appropriate information. Just like every other part, they need to heal from the traumatic incident that caused them to split off.

There are things young parts can (and do) contribute to the System. It's also important they learn and understand and follow the rule that they cannot present (come 'out') at inappropriate times or places if the System is to relate in functional and healthy ways in the outside world. But, because these young parts have needs too, it will be important for the rest of the System to allow these parts to have some 'body time' (time to be out) at pre-arranged times under pre-agreed upon conditions.

Remember to love, to cherish, to value these young parts. Just like the rest of you, they have suffered great wounding, and mustn't be neglected, dismissed, or re-abused within the System. That helps no one; it does not lead to re-integration nor to healing and moving forward.

It can take great patience, finesse and wisdom to deal with wounded 'littles' (young parts) in a System of alters. Yet, as they realize the 'bigs' (older parts) in the System will keep them safe, the rewards are well worth the investment of time and effort as they shed layers of fear and distrust and to learn to be open and loving and inquisitive and playful as they do their own healing work.

.

2 *Ideas, Methods, and Approaches*

The following pages chronicle basic, essential ideas and approaches which other Systems in our sphere of experience have learned, tried, tested, tweaked and fine-tuned.

These ideas and methods have proven themselves to be safe, healthy and effective for working through and recovering from trauma. We have found them to be part of the re-integration work required for managing life successfully as a multiple.

~~The Safe Space/Dome~~

Where you can be safe.

Everyone in the System needs to work together to create a *Safe Space* inside where you all reside. This place is sometimes known as the 'Dome'. This is where parts are when they are not 'out', and is a place to rest, to get to know each other better, and to do your healing work individually and together.

Everyone's mind(s) working together creates your own Dome/Safe Space inside. Using the creative power of your imaginations, you invent this actual place inside of you. Although others will not be able to see your Dome, it is real, nonetheless.

It is very important to create the Dome together, and that it is safe.

Although we will usually call it the Dome here, the Safe Space can take any physical configuration that the System considers safe. Examples include a Sphere, or Pyramid, or Lighthouse, or Cathedral, or Log Cabin, or Tepee, or Space Station. It could be a beautiful place in nature, like a serene ocean shoreline or wildflower prairie or lush rainforest, which is surrounded by a force-field which nothing negative can penetrate. These are only some examples.

Within these guidelines, your 'Dome' can contain within it anything that brings you-all comfort, pleasure, peace and security. Do you want a reading area with a fireplace, an area to play or listen to music, a playground for the littles (young parts)? Would you like to have a perpetual rainbow, or lots of soft, warm blankets and cuddly pillows, or a lake or pool to swim in? Would you like to have unicorns, hummingbirds, butterflies, or a gentle-to-the-System but fiercely protective dinosaur?

You may have it in your Dome.

It is vitally important your Dome (Safe Space) have safety features in place to keep out Dark or negative forces from the outside.

Check the space inside regularly to make certain its integrity has not been breached or compromised, and take immediate action to address and take care of anything that does not look or seem right, or anything that does not belong in your Dome.

Just a note—some Systems put up walls or other barriers in their Dome for reasons of wanting to feel 'safer' or more secure.

The Dome/Safe Space *is already safe* because that is how you-all created it, and because you-all are working to maintain its integrity and safety.

Walls, doors, curtains, fences—anything that can keep you-all from seeing or interacting with each other feeds isolation and separateness—which are either old, dysfunctional patterns or are outmoded safety mechanisms arising out of past experiences. In either case, they will likely create problems down the road, if not now. It's wise to adjust or correct things before they create more difficulties.

There are some drawings of Domes on following pages.

Tepee (Native American) Design Dome
Note: three levels shown

Most domes will have a Lockdown area
(see p. 20 for details)

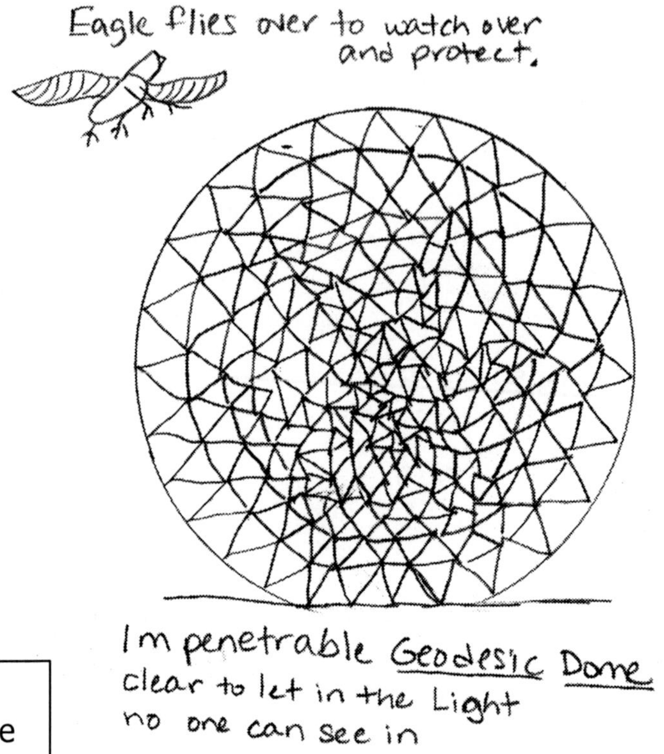

Geodesic Design Dome

Most domes will have a Daily Meeting place (see p. 19)

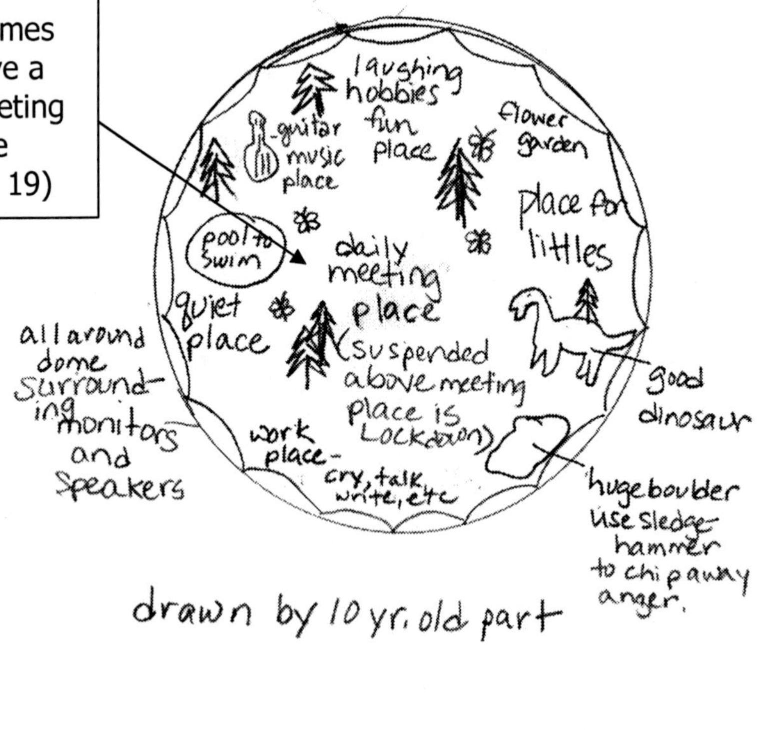

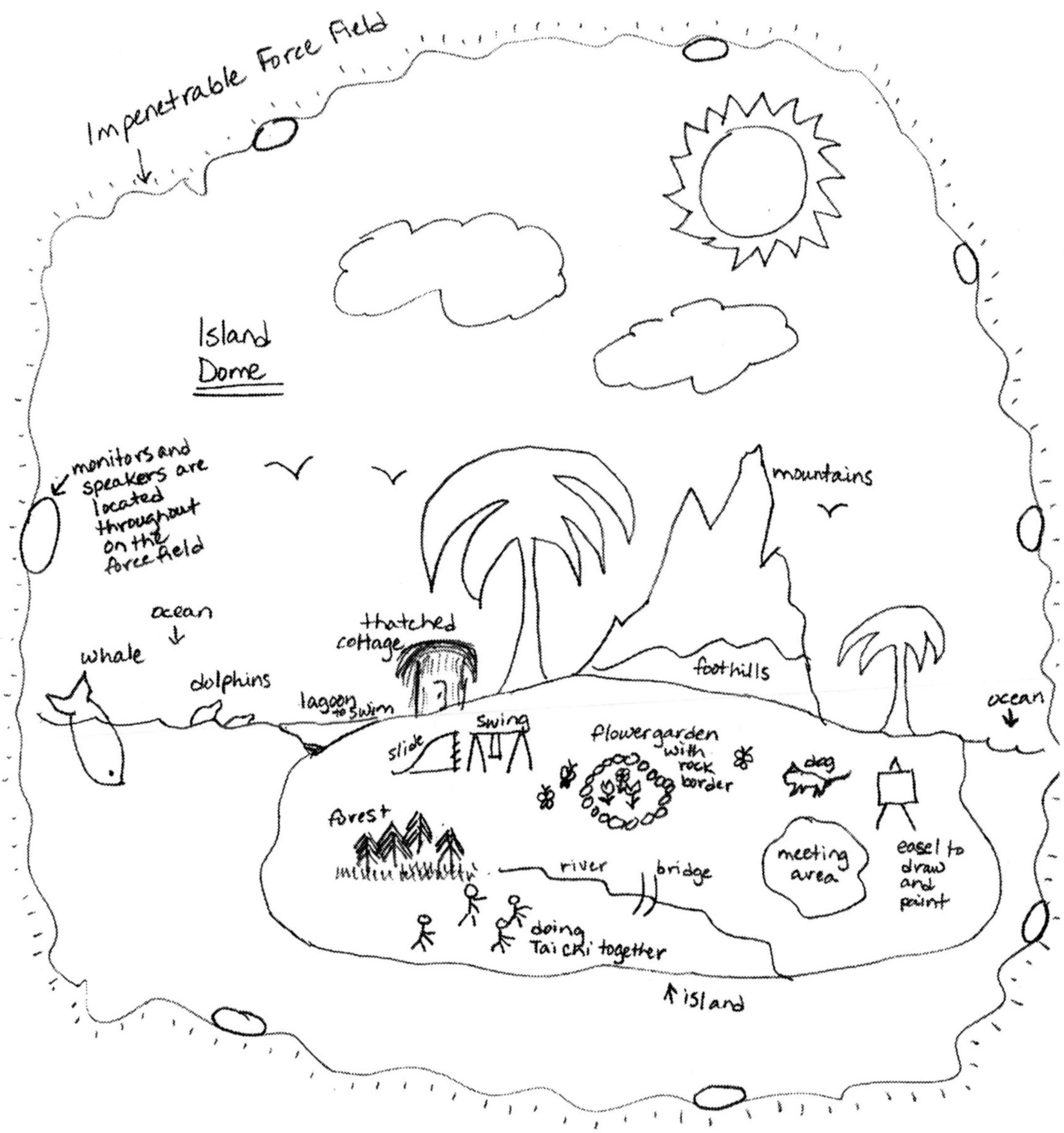

Island Style Dome surrounded by Impenetrable Force Field for safety/privacy. See page 28 for an explanation of the uses of monitors and speakers.

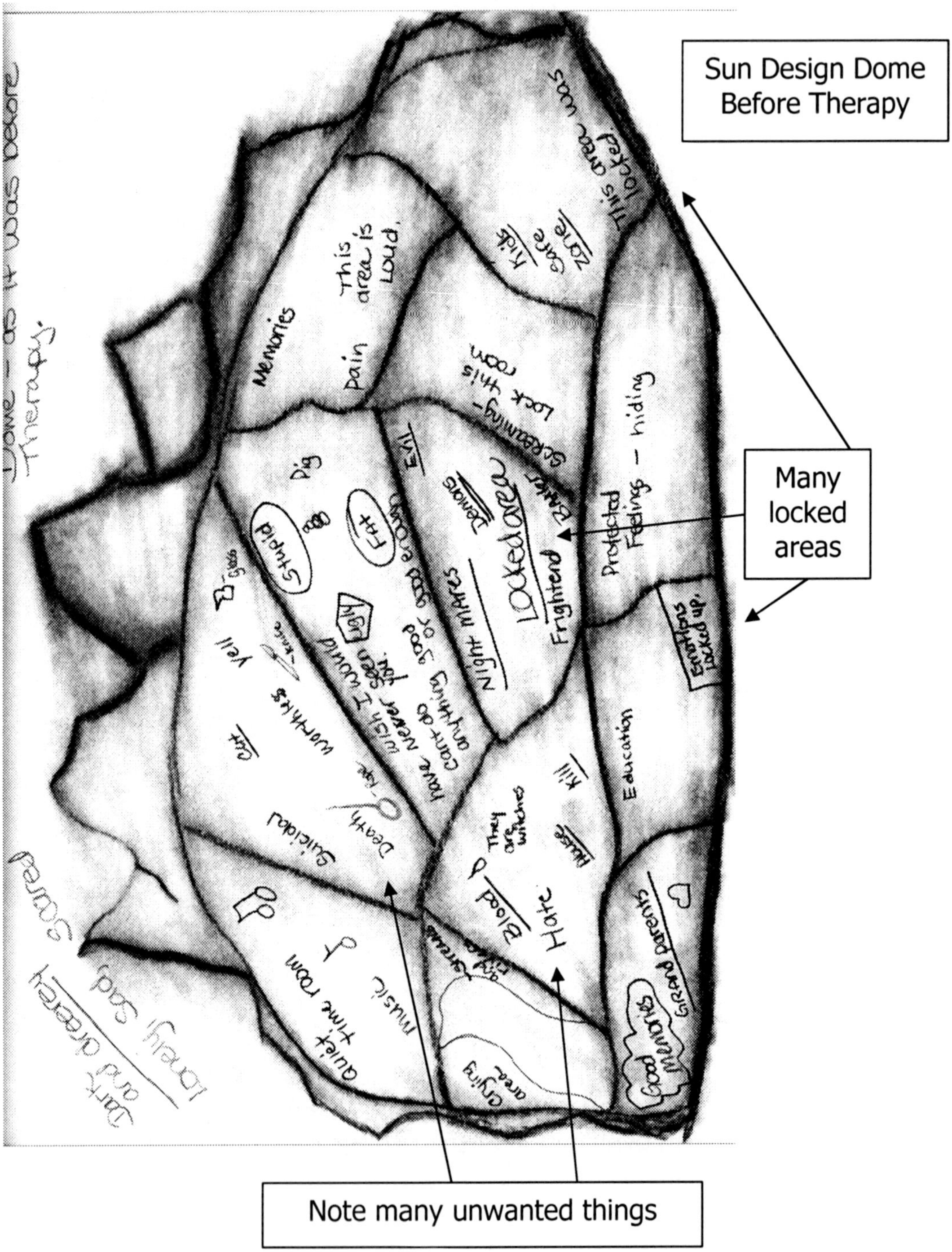
Sun Design Dome Before Therapy
Many locked areas
Note many unwanted things
Dome - as it was before Therapy.
Memories
Pain
This area is loud.
Kids safe zone
This area was locked
Screaming - lock this room
Protected Feelings - hiding
Locked area
Frightend
Night mares
Demons
Evil
Emotions locked up.
Education
Good Memories
Grand parents
Hate
Blood
They are witches
kill
Suicidal
Death
worthless
yell
Stupid
Fat
Ugly
Quiet time room
Music
Dark and dreary
lonely sad
Scared

Sun Design Dome
After Therapy

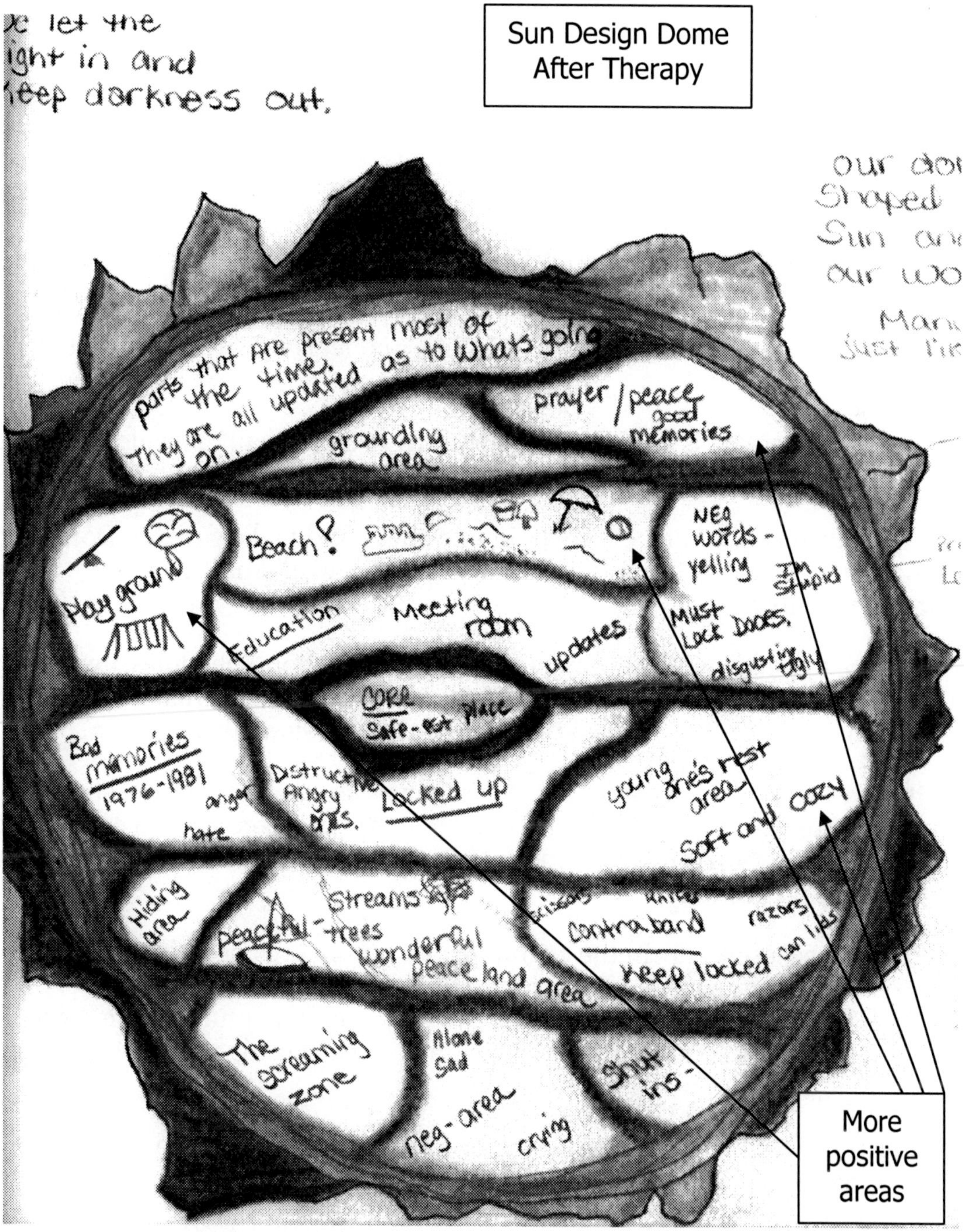

~~Daily meetings~~

At least once a day, every day, there needs to be a 'daily meeting'. Everyone must attend, and everyone is allowed and encouraged to have a voice at these meetings.

The daily meeting can be a time to get to know each other better. It can be a time to check in and see how everyone is doing.

Make sure everyone inside feels welcome, and feels free to share whatever is on their mind.

The daily meeting is a time to talk about what is happening inside and in the outside world.

The daily meeting can be a good time to check and make sure the Dome/Safe Space is clean and clear of intrusions and negativity, and all known parts are all present and accounted for.

Be sure to talk about upcoming events, work or school schedules, appointments, etc. Make sure everyone is aware of what is going on and what needs to happen when. This can help to keep the chaos and confusion down.

If there are ideas, or if there are needs, concerns, problems or questions, now is a good opportunity to voice them and talk about them. Together, you can work to come up with answers or a plan of action. This can be a time to review contracts and create new ones if necessary.

Sometimes, especially in the beginning, as you-all are becoming aware of each other's existence, and getting to know each other—particularly if there is a lot of switching or dissociation occurring—some Systems find it helpful to write down notes of what is talked about in the daily meeting, either during the meeting or after it.

This could be done in the same notebook in which you write to each other; this record could also be a part of your daily journaling.

Also be sure to talk about successes, about good things that are happening, and about things that are going right. It's important to counter-balance what is difficult, painful, frightening, or upsetting with lightness and positiveness and accomplishment.

Did the littles hear a joke they want to tell? Let them. (Be sure to laugh.)

Compliment parts who are working really hard or doing a good job and encourage those who are fearful or sad or struggling or discouraged.

You are a team, and need to work together and help each other. Together you-all are strong. When you are quarreling or not working together it makes everyone weaker, and makes things harder than they would be otherwise; if you are tackling things separately, you may find you are working at cross-purposes and taking more time to achieve some of the same results.

It is helpful to have a 'moderator' who leads the meetings and to rotate this duty so all may have a chance. Note: a moderator is not a dictator or a controller—they simply help keep order and keep the focus on track, they help to make sure everyone who has something to say gets a chance, they can call on parts who haven't talked for a while to see what they are working on or their thoughts about what is being discussed, and so on.

Being the moderator is not about having a personal agenda or not listening to someone or allowing them to talk if they don't particularly like that part, or don't want to hear what that part has to say.

Many Systems find two regular meetings a day, morning and evening, work well. In-between meetings can be held if circumstances warrant them.

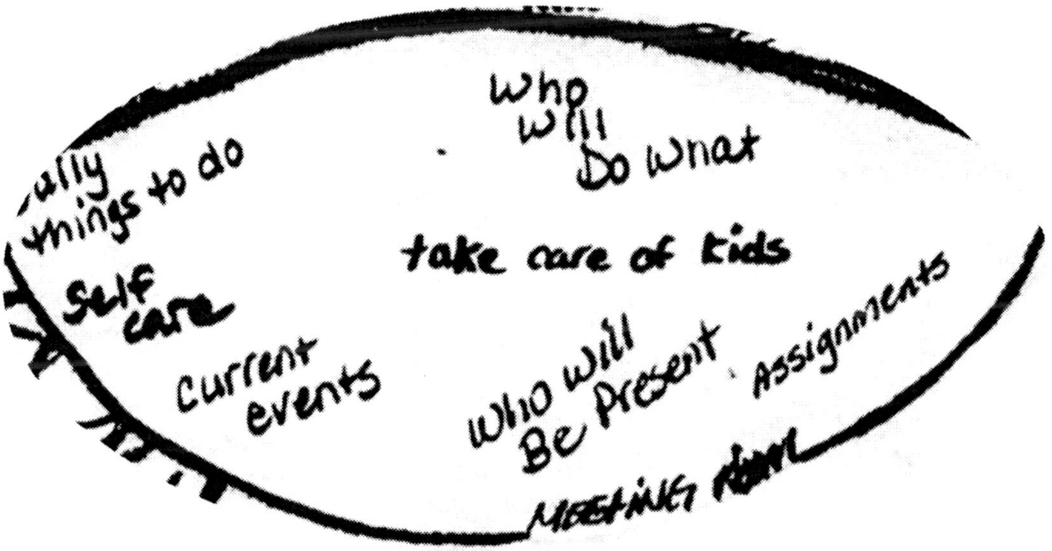

~~Four Commitments to Doing Whatever It Takes to Get Better~~

Having the best outcome requires commitment from all parts to doing whatever it takes to get better.

This includes, but is not limited to:

- Be honest—even when it's hard.

Be honest with yourself, the parts in your System, with your therapist, and with all other health care givers. There is no time for game-playing, and energy is better invested in doing what will move you-all forward in your healing and re-integration.

- Do the work.

It may seem obvious, but if you do not do the work your therapist asks of you, and do not diligently work at the issues that come up along the way, healthy, effective, lasting change is much less likely.

- Cooperate internally.

Having a strong, solid, successful System involves give and take and keeping in mind the larger goals of re-integration and healthy functioning in the inner and outer worlds. When you are a part of any group, including a System of alter personalities, you may not always get your way. It's important to learn to act with integrity, communicate honestly, work to set ego aside, and consider and seek what is for the highest good and in the best interest of the whole System.

- Stand down and step aside.

This is a challenge to controlling, bullying, bossy, fearful, know-it-all, or headstrong parts, or to <u>any</u> part whose speech, behaviors, attitudes, etc. are not in the overall best interest of the System-as-a-whole's healing path. There is no place for Control Freaks, Queen Bees, Lone Rangers, or Loose Cannons in a System.

~~Lockdown~~

"There's Trouble, Right Here In River City."

Sometimes there are parts who, for a variety of reasons, do not want to get better, or who are not willing to do the work it takes to get better. It is important to have a workable and enforceable plan for containing/restraining parts who are not willing to work or cooperate internally. There is also no place in the System for Nay-sayers, Saboteurs, and other Riff-raff. Do not negotiate with parts who are 'terrorists'. If parts are creating chaos and havoc inside and/or outside, if they refuse to work together with other parts, if they won't do their own individual healing work, they need to be contained in some way so their selfishness and negativity do not contaminate and derail the entire System. This is sometimes called 'lockdown'.

The form of the lockdown can vary from System to System, depending upon the System and upon the situational need and the reason why the part (or parts) needs to be contained/restrained.

Lockdown might take a form something like a jail. It might simply be an enclosed area with unbreakable, one way see-thru, sound-proofed glass where the part can see what is going on in the rest of the Dome/Safe Space but other parts cannot see the part being restrained and get distracted or feel sympathetic and allow that part to come out.

Parts cannot be let out unless or until the entire System agrees, along with the therapist, that the part being contained is no longer a danger to themselves, to other parts, or to the System's progress. They are not allowed out to attend the daily meetings.

Another form lockdown can take is to have all the other parts in the System form themselves into a circle around the disruptive part and shower them with love and light and positiveness until this has the effect of breaking through whatever is causing the disruptive, negative part to act out.

Sometimes a part can go into 'seclusion' where they voluntarily agree to 'time out'—spent alone by themselves within the Dome to explore why it is they are choosing to create havoc for others, and resisting doing their own work.

Putting a part in the more extreme forms of lockdown is a regrettable and sad, but sometimes necessary course of action.

Perhaps the parts in lockdown will be able to come out later if their attitude or behaviors change, perhaps not. In either case, the System needs to keep forging ahead, and doing the trauma recovery and re-integration work. Having a part in lockdown does not keep the rest of you from functioning, from doing your own individual and System healing work, or from moving ahead.

~~Addressing Secondary Treatment Issues~~

Sometimes individual parts have addictions—alcohol, nicotine, caffeine, drugs (street drugs or prescription drugs), sex, gambling, shopping, excessive cleaning, being a workaholic, excessive exercising, diet/weight loss aids, etc. Even such things as worry, chaos, crisis, and the need to exert control (over self, others, or situations), can be insidious addictions.

Other parts may have compulsions to self-mutilate or otherwise cause self-harm to the body. Still others might have panic or anxiety attacks, phobias, eating disorders, obsessive-compulsive behaviors (OCD) or other issues. Still other parts may battle clinical depression.

It is important to the whole System's health and well-being to work on these very real problems.

If there are medical problems, these require monitoring, attention and treatment as well.

Healing from trauma, re-integration, and moving forward must include addressing all the issues that will help to keep the System (all the parts inside), as well as the physical body that houses them, moving toward the best possible mental and physical and emotional health.

~~Contracts~~

A contract is a written agreement about a behavior which either needs to happen or must not happen. Contracts need to be specific and detailed, need to have no loop-holes, need to have a time frame for the contracted behavior (it could be an ongoing contract with no expiring date), and the contracts need to be signed by everyone in the System. Depending on the individual System, it may be helpful to list consequences for parts who make the choice to break contracts, and have the rest of the System enforce these consequences.

A System may need more than one contract.

Do not feel badly for needing one or more contracts. Acknowledging there are dysfunctional behaviors that require changing is actually a good sign. It means the System is taking a mature, honest, hard look at itself, and making the choice to move forward to a healthier, more functional place.

Sometimes contracts need to be in place, not because a part is doing something 'bad' or dysfunctional, or abusive to self or System, but out of respect to the overall needs of the rest of the System.

An example of this could be a gay alter agreeing to not engage in gay sexual behavior with someone outside the System if that behavior might cause difficulties for the rest of the System (inside or out). The gay part may not be doing something 'wrong', but may need to realize in some instances that the needs of the many may outweigh the needs of the one. (This isn't necessarily 'fair', but it may need to be this way nonetheless. Welcome to the World of Multiplicity...)

Offer your help, support and encouragement to those inside who are struggling to keep their contracts. Their success is not just an individual victory, but a success for the entire System.

Hold other parts accountable for their speech and behaviors and for keeping their contracts—and know they will hold you accountable as well. Do this in a firm and loving but non-shaming way.

It is also important to share your contract(s) with your therapist. This helper needs to know the areas you are struggling with in order to help you. You might also consider sharing with others you can trust. They can be allies, encouraging you and helping you-all to stay on track.

~~Ever-Increasing Co-Consciousness~~

Co-consciousness comes as all parts become ever-more aware of and share what is going on inside the System, as well as become aware of and share what is happening day to day in the outside world.

Something which other Systems have found to help increase co-conscious awareness is to have monitors and speakers inside the Dome. This allows parts who are inside the Safe Space to remain aware of what is happening outside, such as where you are at, who you are with, what's going on, and so on.

At bad times, the monitors and speakers can be turned off during a particularly distressing event (say, a doctor visit)—just make sure they are turned back on afterwards; or have a plan so only certain parts who can handle the event are able to hear and view it. The event can then be discussed in safe and appropriate ways with the entire System later, during the daily meeting.

An essential component of co-consciousness requires knowing who is present (out). This point may seem obvious, but it is crucial.

Parts inside need to be aware of and know who is 'out' at all times; they also need to know and be able to identify who they are as well. If asked (by your therapist, or by someone in your DID group—in other words, by someone who has a legitimate need or reason to know), the part who is out needs to know, *and be willing to answer* the question "Who's here?" or "Who am I talking with?"

"I don't know" or "nobody" are not acceptable answers unless this is a previously-unknown-to-the-System alter. Parts may hesitate to identify themselves because they do not think they know the 'right answer' to 'who's here?' There might be several reasons for this hesitation, including parts who are out when they ought not to be or are doing something they shouldn't be doing. Parts may try to make excuses. The 'right' answer to the questions above is the honest answer. The System can always deal then with what is going on and who is out. Shyness, game-playing, or simply 'being confused' are not going to help you-all to get healthier nor aid in re-integration.

3 Self Care

Self Care...Self Care...Self Care... The importance of self care cannot be stressed enough. Good self care is absolutely critical for your recovery.

This therapeutic healing work—recovering from trauma, and learning how to manage your multiplicity and the work to re-integrate your System—is the hardest, most grueling, most painful work you will ever do. It is also what will give you the greatest chance at a better, healthier, more satisfying, and functional life.

Taking good care of body, mind and spirit is a critical factor in how the rest of your healing work goes.

If you are not used to taking good, well-rounded care of yourself, you may not be certain what self care involves. Here is a list of some things that self care includes:

- Commitments to not attempt or commit suicide; commitments to no self-violence, and no self-harming behaviors.
- Proper nutrition and the right amount of food for good health.
- Adequate rest and enough sleep.
- Good, basic hygiene and grooming.
- Seeking medical attention when it becomes necessary, and taking medically required drugs as prescribed (not stashing them, failing to take them, or altering the prescribed dosage), and not misusing or abusing drugs, alcohol, or any mind-altering substances.
- Establishing and maintaining a safe, clean, pleasant living environment.
- Having or developing a network of safe, supportive people.
- Learning safe, healthy ways to relax and to reduce and manage stress.
- A regular program of physical activity and exercise appropriate to the physical body's current condition, abilities, and the System's interests.
- Finding or creating opportunities to nourish wounded spirit and emotions.
- Cultivating time and opportunities for fun activities, hobbies, and for play.

Self care includes the general goal of regarding and treating your body in a loving and tender and gentle way and learning to respect 'the skin you're in', especially if this not something you are accustomed to doing; a sometimes forgotten aspect of self-care may include a program of (ahem) 'personal self intimacy'.

Therapeutic Benefits of Outside Interests and Activities

A very important part of your healing process is to participate in activities that bring you meaning, or peace, or good feelings, or help build you up. Seemingly small, simple activities can produce great benefits, including increased self-esteem, self-confidence, and feelings of self worth and well-being; and sometimes these 'smaller' goals are more easily achieved.

Interests and activities outside of therapy help trauma recovery and re-integration to lose some of their overwhelming nature and puts them into a perspective of being only parts of the rest of your life and the life you are creating for yourselves.

Increased social contact helps to combat depression and fights against the desire to isolate ones' self. A network of safe, healthy contacts can widen your support base when you need companionship, or someone to bat ideas around with—not necessarily about anything related to therapy. It helps to have someone to laugh with or share something in common. You can draw strength from other people.

Volunteering can do wonders to boost self-esteem as you realize that, in the middle of all this hard healing work you are doing in therapy, you can still reach out beyond your own pain and do something for someone else.

In most activities, there is generally some level of physical movement /activity/exercise. This can provide health benefits, and improve your overall fitness in ways other than an exercise routine.

Activities could include coaching a softball or Little League or soccer team; having a pet, or pet-sitting for others; building or refinishing furniture; belonging to the quilting group at the local church or attending Wednesday night bingo at the auxiliary, being a part of a book club; taking a yoga or Tai Chi class; attending some form of organized worship services; volunteering at your child's school, or at a local organization whose work you believe in... these are only a few examples.

Calculated challenges, like calculated risks, can lead to growth, progress, success—which leads to taking on other challenges, which lead to growth, progress, more success, which leads to... taking on still other challenges, which leads to more growth, progress, and success, which leads to... Challenging one's self and learning and growing creates an upward spiral of positive expansion of health and well-being, instead of a downward spiral of negativity and isolation.

Self Care and Boundaries

Self care also involves setting appropriate and healthy boundaries and the sometimes difficult choice of avoiding people or places which are abusive, toxic, unhealthy, negative, dysfunctional, or which will undermine the System's progress.

Sometimes this relates to one's own issues.

For instance, if a part has an addiction to alcohol, and has made the healthy choice not to drink, it would be more difficult to keep this contract/self care boundary if they work as a bartender or bar waitress, or are at places with family, friends, or co-workers where alcohol is being served.

Though it would not be impossible to remain non-drinking, until self and System are healthier and more re-integrated, being in environments where alcohol is sold or served might not be the healthiest choice.

Likewise, there is no good reason to continue to choose to be around or interact with (except minimally, if absolutely necessary) people who do not practice their own healthy behaviors. You do not have to remain in the company of people who disrespect you or who treat you neglectfully or are abusive.

Sometimes this self care issue relates more to what is external to us.

Though not always the case, sometimes people around us, even the ones who say they love us and only want the best for us, in fact do not want us to change or get healthy. Though hard to understand and accept, there are reasons this can be true.

As people get healthier, they make changes that reflect they are no longer satisfied living and believing and behaving as they did before. Those who live with them or interact closely with them are then faced with having to adjust and change, too. It will change the status quo, and likely the comfort levels of everyone. Almost all change brings with it an uncomfortable transition time both for the person making the change, and for those around them. Some people are unwilling (for a variety of reasons) to accept the changes and new choices we are making. Sometimes these changes—even though they are healthy ones—might be so disconcerting and upsetting to relationships that others may be unsupportive, or even consciously or unconsciously sabotage the new situation.

The fact that others may not know for certain we are multiple can complicate matters. All the same, the dynamic remains the same whether a person is DID or not. *We have a right to choose not to jeopardize our healing and re-integration to accommodate someone else's comfort level.*

As hard as it may be to remember and to act on this, *you-all have a right to do whatever it is you need to do to get better as long as it is not abusive to anyone else*.

Other important components of self care and boundaries

Making self care your first priority

This is not selfish, regardless of what you may believe or what you may have been told. It also does not imply you should neglect your children, spouse or partner, family pet, job, or other obligations.

However, if you do not give top priority to good care of your physical, mental, emotional, and spiritual health, you will not have the reserves needed to do your healing and recovery and System re-integration work; nor will you have the wherewithal to be there for anyone else in your life. These inner reserves depend on your strength, stamina, resiliency, and inner clarity and calmness.

Doing this therapeutic work takes a lot out of a person—although of course, in the end, you are healthier and more 'filled up' with what will enable you to create a better life for yourselves. As you take ever-better care of yourselves, and progress in your recovery, you will perhaps be able to spread yourself more into other areas.

In the beginning and until you are more stable, it's important to make choices that do not put your health, safety, and progress in jeopardy, and it is especially critical to set what boundaries you need to in order to stay on track with health and recovery.

You need to set limits and learn to say "no"—and being able to stick with your "no" under pressure.

This can be very, very hard to do sometimes. Sometimes we are so entrenched in old habits of always saying "yes", always doing, always volunteering to take things on, always accommodating others, always being 'on', always feeling the pressure (from without or within) to 'perform', that we may not realize today we have the choice available to us to decline these things.

Old habits may be rooted in the need to stay safe, to feel in control, or to believe we are important, or to make other people think we are 'good' or 'ok' or 'make them like us'. It feels really good to feel needed and important and indispensable, especially if those are not things which you necessarily believe about yourself.

Most of us do not like to disappoint other people, or have them be angry or upset with us. Yet as we set boundaries and say "no" if that is what we need to do, sometimes that happens.

Hopefully, however, as you continue to do this healing work, you will come to understand you-all have intrinsic worth separate from what you do (or don't do), the roles you take on (or choose to not take on), and how other people regard you.

It really is ok to take care of yourself, including not over-extending yourselves. It is ok to begin to set boundaries. It is ok to say no sometimes. It is not just ok, but necessary to set limits.

Though it is important to resist giving in to pressure to go against your boundaries, it is also important to remember boundaries are not set in stone. They are there to protect your progress toward health. Boundaries sometimes shift over time, depending on your well-being and where you are on your life and healing path. Boundaries may need to be tighter or more strict in the beginning as you practice setting and keeping them, and as others are getting used to your different choices and behaviors. Some time down the road, you may be able to set boundaries with less rigidity and more balance.

It may take some time to learn what your limits are. Be gentle and patient with yourself during this learning process. This is like learning any new skill—it takes time, and there is a learning curve—and there are likely to be errors in judgment along the way. Don't give up... keep after it. With practice, this process has the potential to get somewhat easier and more natural after a while.

Medical/Health Care Issues

Good care of the physical body is very important to your overall recovery. The physical body has need for more than just food and water, rest and sleep, exercise and physical activity, clothing and shelter. The physical body also requires attention and monitoring in order to maintain energy and vitality and good health. Sometimes there are medical conditions such as asthma, high blood pressure, high cholesterol, heart conditions, diabetes, ulcer, or such, which require treatment.

Sometimes past trauma issues make seeing a health care provider (doctor, dentist, eye doctor, gynecologist, internist, physical therapist...) or having medical tests or procedures done, very, very difficult because of triggers, fears, or trust issues.

It is very important—for a number of reasons—for your health care provider(s) to know of your diagnosis. Especially early in your healing process, or if there is a lot of uncontrolled switching, or until your System has a good amount of co-consciousness and is working well together, knowing your diagnosis (DID) can be valuable (and enlightening) information for your practitioner who may be baffled by seeming inconsistencies or other phenomena which will make more sense once they have this additional information. Once they realize they are treating one physical body, but perhaps more than one patient, and as they learn a few basic things about DID, they can move toward a better understanding of how to best serve your over-all, (collective) health care needs.

If your clinician is not familiar with dissociative disorders, and with DID in particular, you might want to enlist the help of your therapist in briefly explaining the basics to him or her if you are at a loss to answer their questions or concerns. You will need to sign a release of information for this.

The step of revealing this intimate piece of information involves taking a calculated risk, but remember these are individuals who (should) have your welfare and best interests in mind, and the dividends realized from disclosing this information can be worth taking the risk.

Remember that health care professionals are bound by confidentiality and a professional code of ethics. Remember too, you have done nothing wrong, and you do not have any reason to be ashamed.

It has proven helpful for other Systems to have a standard letter written for all your health care providers—ones you see presently, and any new providers you may see in the future. This letter will, among other things, tell them your diagnosis (Dissociative Identity Disorder—'multiple personalities'), and if there is a secondary diagnosis, such as Post Traumatic Stress Disorder; it will also inform them about your trauma history, and if that manifests in any ways that would be helpful for them to know so they can better work with you.

In this letter, you can also mention any special needs or concerns you have, and let them know what you need from them to make medical/health care appointments (exams, procedures, etc.) easier so you can take the best care of your body's health that you are capable of taking. (There are a couple sample letters in Appendix B. They can give you ideas how to write to your own medical/health care providers, and things you might say. They are only examples; you can tailor them to your own particular needs and situations, or write an entirely different letter.)

Most doctors and health care providers are pleasantly surprised and appreciative of your candor and your proactive approach to taking care of yourselves.

One idea for handling the stressor of medical appointments and treatment might be to ask an understanding and supportive friend or family member who knows your diagnosis to accompany you to office visits and appointments for medical procedures. Let your health care provider know this ahead of time, and why you need this, and seek their permission and cooperation in this being allowed. Many doctors are sympathetic, and do not have a problem in accommodating this request within reason.

A plan that has been of great benefit to other Systems is to find who inside is best capable of ensuring medical/health care needs are being taken care of. This designated part will be the one who goes to all medical appointments, the one who will communicate with health care providers, and the one to undergo exams and procedures. Other parts must agree not to come out during medical visits/procedures, and must agree not to interfere with or block or hinder the part who has agreed to fill this role on behalf of the System. You may need to write up a contract to this effect, and have everyone in the System sign the contract.

Look for a part who has suffered no primary trauma, or whose therapeutic issues do not involve medical/body-care triggers or fears or anxieties or other related difficulties. It could also be a part who has already worked through trauma-triggers that might still impede others in the System from being able to take care of medical/health needs. This is an instance where we recommend that one part takes on the role, and other agree not to interfere.

This is a critical agreement to work out and implement. There can be potentially tragic consequences to violating such an agreement, or not having one in the first place. There was an instance we heard of, where an adult part in a System was undergoing a surgical procedure, and in the middle of surgery, a young, frightened, triggered part came out and began tearing out IVs and becoming combative with the doctor. This person did not have a workable plan, and the doctor was unaware of the diagnosis of DID because the person chose not to share it. The doctor refused to continue to treat this person, feeling he had been misled, and therefore been exposed to unnecessary risk and liability.

Such chaos and potentially dangerous behavior—with very serious medical and psychological consequences—can be avoided by the System recognizing what needs to happen and being willing to adhere to appropriate agreements.

Another similar good idea is to have one designated part who is the only one responsible for taking/ingesting necessary medications (in any form). This can help to ensure needed medicines (including nutritional supplements like vitamins, and over-the-counter medicines) are taken for certain and not forgotten, and that doses are not doubled or tripled because multiple parts are taking it on themselves to administer the meds and may not have realized the dose had already been taken.

Time Management

Considering the fact that a lot of non-DID folks have difficulty managing their time, it is not surprising with the added factor of being multiple and all that entails, conscious and effective use of time can be even more challenging, and by extension, even more important.

We have multiple selves coexisting within the one body. In the beginning, some don't even know others exist, and those aware of each other may be in conflict. Some alters may operate from old patterns of fear, self-reliance, distrust, and/or dissociating. You-all may lose whole blocks of time you are unable to account for. All in all, it's easy to understand why DID folk need to think about creating and using solid time-management skills workable for their particular System.

Things can get easier as the System becomes more aware of who all is a part of it, begins to get to know and trust each other and learns to work ever better together. You find workable plans for managing what is required for healing from trauma, and for re-integration. You can better work on meeting life's demands.

Here are a few tried and tested suggestions and strategies that can help you-all begin to get a better handle on managing your time.

In the beginning, keeping a log of your day, what's going on hour by hour, (talked about in more detail on page 45), can give you insights into where the System is right now in terms of co-conscious awareness, activities of daily living, time management, if you are 'losing time', and so on.

Another helpful time management tool the System can put into place is to have some type of record keeping system using a calendar book, or Day-Timer™ type book. It does not have to be expensive or fancy—just so long as it has plenty of room to write. A spiral bound notebook can be organized to work just as well.

All the System commitments including school assignments, work schedules, when bills are due, appointments, meetings and deadlines—everything that is important to remember gets recorded in this book, regardless of which alter actually goes to work or to school, or pays the bills, or attends the appointments. It is best to write things down as soon as you learn of them so you do not forget to write them down later. Something noted by another part is not necessarily easy to remember; everyone writing things down in the Time Planner rather than relying on their (or any other part's) memory, ensures everything gets documented in the Planner, and thereby stands a greater likelihood of accomplishment.

The Time Planner is also a place to write out daily goals and plans for what needs to be accomplished. This can include dropping off the dry cleaning, returning library books by their due date, picking up the kids from school, calling the plumber, grocery shopping, taking the cat to the vet for her annual checkup, baking cupcakes for your son's birthday party at school, calling in a prescription for renewal, and so on.

Though these may seem like simple, straightforward, easy to remember things, matters are neither simple nor straightforward when you are DID.

Anything that needs to happen gets recorded and put on 'the schedule'. This way, things are not forgotten, and priorities for doing things can be established.

The way the System organizes their personal Time Planner is up to them. There is no right or wrong. It comes down to whatever is easiest for a particular System to understand. Devise one best suited to ensure that you-all record dates in a manner enabling you to run your life as smoothly as possible.

As things are accomplished, they can be checked off. Applaud yourselves for accomplishments and for getting things done. This is no small feat! Use your daily meeting to celebrate successful use of this tool to keep surprise, chaos, crisis, etc. down to a minimum.

The Time Planner is a tool that works if parts are talking and working together, sharing information instead of withholding it. It can be sabotaged if one misplaces or hides the book. Depending on the circumstances, or the parts in one's System, it might be worth writing up a contract to always keep the book in the same place—a place which is safe, which is easy to remember and which is known to all parts, and to which you all have access.

Consulting the time planner during the daily meeting can prove helpful.

Another tool you can use to work toward more successful time management is to develop regular routines. Though it is critical to learn to be flexible, there is also value in routine. Routines can change as needed—such as a somewhat different routine during the school year as opposed to one during the summer.

Routines can give one a template around which one's days can be shaped, and this can give a real sense of security and anchoring.

A routine can be as simple as getting up at the same time each morning and going to bed at the same time each night, brushing your teeth after breakfast and supper, having morning and evening System meetings, checking to make certain the Dome is 'clean' from negativity and anything that does not belong, eating two or three meals during the day, having a regular time set aside to journal or collage, making it a point to do soft stretching exercises before bed, and so on.

Individual Systems can work to find their own routines, their own rhythms,—whatever best suits their individual/System needs and is most helpful.

Some things are more difficult to put into strict schedules, but as long as these needed things are being recorded into the System's Time Planner, they are more likely to get done than if they are unrecorded and left to memory or to chance.

Coach Yogi Berra said "If you don't know where you are going, you are likely to end up somewhere else." This is also true when it comes to managing one's time.

Although circumstances outside of one's control will always come up, it also comes back to choices and accountability. If you-all are taking proactive approaches to taking care of things, and if you have a plan on how you are going to fill your day(s), you are much more likely to succeed in managing your time, and having perhaps better outcomes, than if you just let the day happen around you.

~~What Else Does It Take?~~

What else does it take to successfully heal from trauma, re-integrate, and navigate life as a multiple?

Show up and do the work

While this may seem obvious, it is sometimes overlooked or not given enough credit. If you don't show up for and participate in the daily meetings, if you don't get to know and develop trust for and work with the others inside, if you avoid working on your own trauma issues (which caused you to split off in the first place), if you are not *actively, consciously, purposefully doing the work every day,* it is highly probable you will not move forward from where you are into a better, more satisfying place of your own choosing.

Flexibility and Creativity

These are two highly valuable life-skills to cultivate. Despite one's best laid plans and hardest work, life, circumstance, and people are unpredictable. Life is often not fair. Life is hard. Change is hard. Healing is hard. Being DID is challenging. People we interact with can be abusive, hurtful, neglectful, oblivious, fickle, maddening, insensitive, without understanding. Problem-solving is sometimes difficult or distasteful. Sages from Buddha to TV news-journalist Walter Cronkite have told us "that's the way it is". And it's true.

The tools in our internal tool box can help us (both those who are DID and those who are not DID) through life challenges, are the ability to be flexible, and the ability to get creative when the need calls for it.

We are wiser than we often give ourselves credit for. We also have an entire System of alters with ideas, strengths, and insights to draw upon.

Often, too, we can sometimes find ways through difficult situations by shifting our viewpoint or approach.

Pacing and Balance

There can be a powerful urge/draw to want to "hurry up and get done with all this therapy work"—a desire to be rid of the accompanying pain that goes with recovery, the grieving of losses, and the acknowledgement that you are multiple and are going to be multiple for the rest of your life.

It's also very common to think this work shouldn't take as long as it sometimes does.

Sometimes the rush to be done comes at the expense of not truly spending the time and effort required for the healing work and the accompanying System-work. Alternately, sometimes you can get so immersed in always working on your 'therapy issues' and DID issues that you forget that there is more to life than healing and re-integration.

Pacing oneself, and seeking healthy balance are two other very important life-skills.

A sense of humor is invaluable to this work

If you can't laugh at life, and at yourselves from time to time, you'll doom yourself to a much gloomier, lonelier existence than if you can find humor along the way. Sometimes the littles (young parts) in the System can help the bigs (older parts) to find humor, surprise, laughter, and play as you go along. And sometimes older parts can help young ones to do this.

4 Therapeutic Approaches

~~Trauma Recovery/DID Re-Integration~~

A few things involved in trauma recovery/DID re-integration work are:

Your therapist might ask you to keep a daily journal about things that happened to you in the past, and about specific topics which your therapist may suggest, or about what is going on for you-all right now.

Be prepared that each part will need to do their own journaling, at least about past issues and about their own individual thoughts and beliefs and experiences. One alter does not journal for the entire System. Do not presume you can speak honestly and fully for any other part.

Yes, this does take more time and work. And yes, it is necessary for each part to do their own work on their individual healing as well as System-work. And no, you don't have to like it, but that's what it takes.

Other assignments might include making collages, drawing or painting, or sculpting with clay.

Sometimes writing or drawing with your non-dominant hand can help facilitate getting words or feelings out when you are having a hard time getting started, or are feeling 'stuck'.

One creative assignment given to a System was to dig a flower bed—not just by hand, *but with a spoon*—and as they did so, to water the ground with their tears, their vomit, their screams, their cries, their prayers, and whatever else poured forth from them as they were working...and then to plant seeds, care for them tenderly, and watch them grow and flourish into beauty and new life...

...what a marvelous, ingenious use of pent-up emotions and energy! What a wonderful metaphor for the healing process!

Sometimes dance movement therapy or movement work can help to get memories and feelings out of your body and provide surprising insights and results, especially if you are not used to being 'in your body'.

Likewise, sometimes massage or other types of body-work can be helpful in releasing stored tension and body memories.

Because these types of therapeutic-healing work can sometimes be triggering, it is essential this is done with a safe person in a safe environment, and you have support arranged for afterward in the event it is needed. This might be another example of a short time span during which the monitors and speakers in the Dome/Safe Space might need turned off, remembering, of course, to turn them back on after the session is over.

~~Emotional Release Work~~

Emotional release work can be helpful in expressing powerful (and sometimes scary-feeling) emotions through vocalization—yelling, screaming, cussing, or just saying what is pent up inside and you've never been allowed to say, or what you've never allowed yourself to say—or what's never been safe to say.

Release work might involve working to allow yourself to cry the tears you might never have been allowed to cry before and to let whatever sounds feel right to come out when you cry. It is ok to make whatever sounds you want to make, without believing you must stifle the sounds or the tears—and without holding back.

Release work might involve tearing up telephone books, or beating on telephone books with a foam bat. While this might feel awkward or intimidating or scary at first, your therapist is there to support you and to make sure it is a therapeutically safe and healing experience.

Release work is often something that does not come easily, or quickly. It can feel very scary or uncomfortable doing something different, something you have never done before—letting your emotions out. Be patient and gentle with yourself... and keep after it. Effects might be slow in showing, but if you stay with the work, they will come.

It can be very empowering to find your voice, to use it, and to get your horror, pain, rage, grief, terror, and other emotions out in a way that does not harm yourself or anyone else.

In doing movement or body work, or emotional release work, it is very important for the part who is doing that work to stay as present as possible, and not dissociate, (and not to 'bail out' and 'dump' another part in their place there in the release-work session), which only perpetuates the difficulties and distress.

In doing emotional release work, it is important to do it under supervision/ witness of your therapist in the controlled setting of their office space—and not in settings outside the therapy environment where it could create or initiate a whole raft of problems.

Once you finally begin to let the tears, the anger, and all the other pent-up emotions out, it can sometimes feel uncontrollable—like a volcano erupting, or like a dam bursting. It can sometimes make you feel worse, initially, than you did before. This is because you are 'feeling' at last, and not remaining numb to the emotions and feelings that were there all along.

Emotional release work can sometimes make you feel as though you are 'out of control' (at least for a time). There may be fear that if you 'let go', you might not be able to keep on doing what life outside of therapy requires of you when you leave your therapy session. You may feel like these emotions are a bottomless pit and like you may never get it all out. You may believe the emotions you are feeling are so strong they will overwhelm, even harm you. These are normal, if not entirely accurate beliefs.

It is far worse to move through life numb, and on 'automatic pilot', and without feeling the range of emotions that are there to feel; and it is far more dangerous to yourself (and others) to keep things bottled up. It negatively impacts physical and emotional health for ones' self, and it negatively impacts one's relationships. It is far better to release these emotions in a safe and controlled environment rather than have them erupt and disrupt your life at an unexpected, un-chosen, possibly unsafe or unwise moment.

Your therapist is a safe guide/witness/support person while you are doing emotional release work. They are (or should be) trained in how to assist you in staying safe while at the same time getting the most therapeutic benefit from these release work sessions.

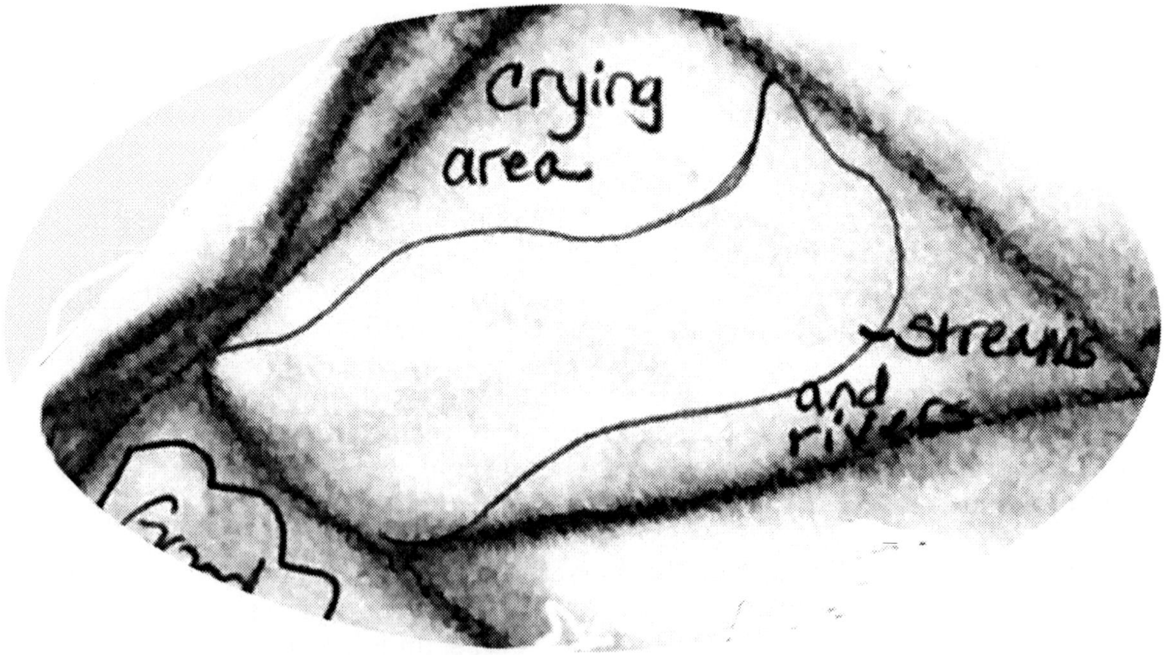

~~The Daily Log~~

Your therapist might also request you keep a log of each day's activities and what all is going on during a day. This can yield information which will be valuable self-knowledge and important information for your therapist.

Examples which might be recorded could include such things as:

- if you aren't able to leave your home, or your room all day;
- or if you haven't had a shower for three days;
- or all you've had to eat all day is a handful of corn chips and four cups of coffee;
- or if someone in your System is bingeing and purging;
- if parts are sleeping all the time, or if no one is able to sleep; if a part in your System spends ten hours every day cleaning a house that's already clean;
- if there hasn't been a System meeting in over a week;
- if you are still in school, or have gone back to school—how are your classes going? How are your study habits? How are your grades? If you work or are employed, how is work going? How's your work attendance? How are your relationships with your boss and co-workers?
- are any utilities up for disconnect because mail isn't being opened or bills not being paid on time?
- is credit card debt climbing because parts are spending recklessly and without others in the System knowing about it?
- are prescribed medications being taken as directed?
- are parts drinking to excess, or using other means to 'self-medicate'?
- are any parts participating in risky sexual behaviors?
- if you are in continual conflict with your spouse or partner or if you're screaming at your kids (inside kids or outside kids);
- if someone in your System is self-mutilating the body (by cutting, scratching, burning, etc)
- if a part is continuing to choose to be with perpetrators or unsafe people
- if it is now 7 p.m. Thursday night, and no one in the System has any recollection of anything since Wednesday morning when you left the house for work...

...these are examples of things your therapist must know in order to help.

The daily log can indicate where contracts may be needed.

It can also indicate if you are having missing, lost, or unaccountable-for time. This is a potentially very serious situation which needs to be addressed with your therapist's help.

If parts are recording things difficult for you (or others) to admit to in the daily log, or telling them to your therapist, do not harass them or complain about them being a 'tattletale'. Healing and re-integration are intertwined, joint ventures, and one part's choices affect all of you. Without honesty, these are pointless exercises.

~~Therapeutic Approaches, and New Techniques and Modalities~~

Techniques and approaches may vary from therapist to therapist depending upon their particular training, and their own beliefs and orientation. It also depends upon their understanding of what it takes to recover from trauma and how to work with those who are DID, and what is required to successfully re-integrate a System of alter personalities.

There are some new, leading edge techniques in trauma recovery.

Therapists must receive training in each of these techniques before using them with clients. These new techniques include:

- EMDR (Eye Movement Desensitization and Reprocessing).
- EFT (Emotional Freedom Therapy)—also known as 'tapping'.
- TIR (Traumatic Incident Reduction).

Although these therapeutic tools have proven helpful for others, **some or all of them might not be appropriate in every case for those who have suffered trauma or who are DID (multiple).**

In order for any of these techniques to be helpful, the System must be able to limit switching. It is essential one part stay present during the time when these techniques are being utilized.

A therapist who is familiar with the techniques, and who has training in them, will be able to judge—based on their knowledge of the client—whether their use might be helpful.

Therapists using EMDR must attain a Level II training before using EMDR with folks who have a dissociative disorder (including DID). In Level II training they learn to administer an evaluative test called DES (and the ADES, used with adolescents), that will detect if the client's level of dissociation is high enough to contraindicate use of EMDR.

Another part of the therapist's discernment must take into account the resiliency of the client.

While these techniques may assist with trauma resolution, they will not impact on your DID diagnosis or the re-integration work that is required for managing your multiplicity.

Ask your therapist about these modalities, or you can find out more information at the library or on the Internet (see Chapter 8)

However, as with all things—whether on the Internet or in life in general—use caution in seeking out the information that interests you. There is good information out there. (The websites of the associations affiliated with these techniques are also in Chapter 8.)

Unfortunately, there is also information which ranges from unhelpful to misleading to strongly biased or following a particular agenda, to outright false. If you access information, be sure to check it out with your therapist. You do not have to believe or buy into all the information on trauma, memory, and DID that exists.

~~DID group~~

Not every therapist has, or is willing to offer, a DID group because they can be fraught with myriad difficulties which would render the group experience more problematic than helpful. Nevertheless, a well-run, well-managed group, facilitated by a therapist with an established history of working with trauma survivors and folks with DID, can often be very helpful.

A group can provide validation and support from persons who are or have been where you are. It can let you know you are not alone in your experience, and your feelings and emotions are normal and ok to feel and express.

The DID group can be a venue where you can find encouragement, ask questions, seek out information, and request feedback.

It can also give you the occasional, but sometimes much needed 'kick in the pants' when you are stalling, resisting, or deflecting from doing the work. It's hard to look someone in the eye and explain why you are not willing to do the hard soul-baring therapeutic work they, and others who are sitting in the same room with you, are doing.

Though nearly everyone feels some degree of resistance and fear about facing difficult, painful, terrifying things, or things they feel ashamed about, it is important to climb off the fence of indecision/safety, and come down either on the side of making the choice to do the work—whatever it takes—and move on, or on the side of choosing to not do the work and settling for staying where you are, and living a life that is less than what may be possible for you (self and System).

There may be times when denial, either about whether your traumatic experience ever happened (or if it was really 'that bad'), or whether you're really DID, or both, will rear its head. This is very common. Hearing feedback from peers sometimes gets through in a different way than hearing it from your therapist.

If there are 'old timers' in the group who have been at this for a while, they will likely have pointers of what has helped them; it can also help to see someone who is further down the path to healing, who is having successes, and who is living proof it can be done.

There are times when it can be painfully hard to listen to others' truths and experiences and to watch and listen as they struggle to share memories and release emotions. It can evoke strong feelings in others within the group.

It can sometimes be hard to stay present and not dissociate—both for the sharer and the listener. There are reasons to work to get beyond this difficulty and challenge.

It can help the person who is sharing to perhaps feel they no longer have to be alone with their trauma experience (or their DID). It can let them know they are accepted (and acceptable) and cared about regardless of what their experience was and where they are at this point in their healing work.

It can also let everyone else in the room know in an experiential way, brave sharing of difficult material is ok—that others are courageously taking the risk to share honestly, and so can they.

It can be profoundly healing to speak your truth and to be heard; it can also be healing to simply be there for another and bear witness to their pain and struggle.

Therapists are your guide through all of this, and a source you can look to for help in staying present for another, and for doing your own sharing.

5 Fallout from Trauma

Triggers, Flashbacks, and Body Memories~~

Other important things to learn about, and find ways to manage are: triggers, flashbacks, and body memories.

Triggers

Triggers are something that remind you of, or bring you back to, an emotional or psychic place of remembering something about the traumatic event(s) in your past.

Triggers vary greatly from person to person, and from alter to alter. A person (or part) may or may not be aware of what their triggers are, or why they are triggers. Triggers are specific to that person's/alter's experience. Something which is very triggering to one person or alter may not be a trigger to anyone else, perhaps not even to anyone else in one's own System. Triggers usually involve one or more of the five senses: sight, sound, taste, touch or smell.

One basic way to begin learning to manage triggers is to have each part make a list of what their triggers are, understanding this list may grow longer as the therapeutic process progresses. This is not because you're 'getting worse', but is because your bank of self-knowledge and self-awareness is growing. This is a good thing, because the more you know, the less chance you have of being blindsided by something in the future.

Each alter can share their list with others inside, and as co-consciousness and the level of trust between parts increases, you-all can find ways of helping each other when one or more parts get triggered.

It will be important to share your lists of triggers with your therapist, who will have additional ideas on how to work to get them to a manageable level. However, please remember there is no magic answer, no quick fix to any of this. It comes down to doing hard and challenging work, seeing what works for others, and sometimes, plain old trial and error.

Another place to get ideas on managing triggers is in your DID group. Talk to your therapist about how to best talk about this in group. Things which trigger one of you may also trigger someone else in the group, but don't let this frighten you off from talking about your triggers. A group is a safe place to talk about issues of all kinds, and to find you are not alone in your triggers, and fears, and struggles. You can often get valuable ideas from others in group on how they successfully handle triggers.

We are not isolated in the effects our triggers have. People around us, and those we are in some type of relationship with are also affected when we are triggered, or when we learn to deal with our triggers.

One System had this to say about triggers...

> "People have different triggers. It would be helpful to discuss these things. I was raped at a baseball field. Someone said something very similar to your statement when that happened.
>
> Allow yourself some room to avoid certain triggers while working on becoming comfortable with a physical environment that has been involved in previous hurts. It's very possible to overcome these triggers with work and support. Believe in yourself!!"

While some triggers may never totally go away, over time you can figure out what works, and so to get to a place where the effects of triggers don't have to be as devastating or disabling.

Flashbacks

Flashbacks are sometimes experienced by people who had been subject to trauma, or witnessed someone else being traumatized.

A flashback is when the memory of the trauma comes back so vividly that the person (or part) actually feels as if they are re-experiencing the event. Flashbacks are exquisitely real feeling and seeming.

Flashbacks are very common in persons who have lived through traumatic experiences, and a common indicator of Post Traumatic Stress. Flashbacks may be frequent before entering therapy, and early in the therapeutic process, but can still occur later, as you are continuing to discover things you may not have remembered before.

When you realize you may be having a flashback, it's important to find ways to remind yourself that's what it is—a flashback, that what seems to be happening right now actually happened in the past, and you are safe now. This is not necessarily something that can be accomplished right away, but is a goal to work for.

Sometimes, it is helpful to ask questions or do things that will give you an external reality check.

It is also important to find ways to be good to and gentle with yourself.

Being in, or having a flashback is a very solitary experience, and can be a vulnerable, frightening time. It's very important to find ways of staying safe during times of flashbacks.

Sometimes, after the flashback is over, you need some time to yourself (though it's important not to become isolated), and sometimes it is helpful to be with or talk with someone you trust, someone who knows about your circumstances, and can be reassuring and supportive and help you to re-ground.

When the flashback is over, it will be very important to ground yourself as much as possible in the present. Do things which will help you to orient to time and place and to help you get grounded and feeling back in your body again. This could include such things as running cool water over your hands, or walking around the place where you are (if it is a safe place). These are things which can get you back in touch with your body in the here-and-now by using some of your senses.

You might want to talk to someone safe about your flashback. You can also talk to yourself, and talk to others inside about where you are at, about what day it is, and other things to work to help you to regain awareness of present reality.

Above all stay safe, and be sure to take good care of yourself. There will be time later to process the flashback by journaling or drawing, talking with other parts inside at the daily meeting, discussing it with your therapist, and in group.

Just like virtually everything else in trauma recovery and DID re-integration work, learning to handle triggers, and learning to handle flashbacks is a process.

As you-all get to know and trust each other, you can learn to help each other when one of you is having a flashback.

It is also a really good idea to come up with a safety/contingency plan for what to do when you or someone in the System is having a flashback. This is perhaps something that could be worked on in the daily meeting, and with the help of your therapist. Asking in group how others cope with flashbacks (during and after) can give you helpful ideas too.

Body Memories

Body memories are similar to flashbacks in the sense your physical body feels the sensations it had during the original episode of trauma. For example, if you suffered a beating or a sexual assault, your body may feel those identical sensations even though you are not being beaten or assaulted right now.

At a cellular level, the body stores a memory of everything it has experienced. Sometimes this is evoked through touch, ranging from casual touch, to intimate touching, to massage and body-work. Sometimes a trigger can cause these body memories to break through.

Sometimes the body memory just surfaces. Although there are times when a body memory coincides with an identifiable flashback, sometimes it may seem to happen 'out of nowhere'.

This can be extremely frightening and unnerving, especially if you don't know this is what is happening. It does not mean you have 'lost it' or that you are crazy. Your mind is not playing a cruel trick on you, but rather is presenting you with memory or information that needs to be worked through so you can heal from the wounding you experienced.

The phenomena of flashbacks and body memories can become more complex when you are not the only personality residing within your physical body—especially until you-all each have a greater sense of 'self' and 'System'.

If you have not yet reached a place of distinguishing between yourself and others in your System, you may have a consciousness of sensations that are the memory and/or current experience of another part. While this may seem strange or odd, it is not unheard of.

Each part doing their own work, getting to know each other better, and getting strong senses of self- and System- is really what will get things to a more manageable place.

6 Relating to Others

~~Disclosure~~

The topic of disclosure is important to talk about inside and to do some advance thinking and planning before you actually make the decision whether or not to disclose your diagnosis (DID) to someone else.

There are thoughts and ideas about disclosure scattered throughout *got parts?,* as seem applicable within specific sections. Some of the main thoughts are gathered here so you can consider them within one section.

Though not always an easy thing to do, nor necessarily an advisable thing to do on an indiscriminate or widespread basis, there are instances where it may be important to reveal the fact of your multiplicity to someone in your life. Nearly without exception, it will be very important for you to let all your health care providers know you are DID, and what that entails.

Disclosure should be a System decision.

One question you might want to think about, and talk over inside, is what you-all might stand to gain or lose by disclosing, and why you are thinking of disclosing to a particular individual. Writing these things down may help you to see them outside of yourself which can be a helpful tool when faced with having to make a decision about something.

Here are some points to consider about disclosure. As with potentially anyone you might disclose your multiplicity to, there may be those who will be understanding and compassionate and helpful and supportive. Others may not behave in any of these ways.

There are still many mental health professionals who either do not believe DID is real, or do not have up-to-date and relevant information about its accurate diagnosis, how it manifests, nor how multiplicity can be successfully managed and Systems re-integrated. Therefore, it's easy to understand why the average person does not really understand DID either. People whom we encounter may have strong—though often mistaken—beliefs about multiple personalities. They may have their own fears, prejudices, misunderstandings and misconceptions, some of which may have been fueled by television, movies and books, and the Internet.

They might not understand what DID really is, or not take the time to get to understand it, and presume we are unstable, unreliable, we may not be able to hold down a job, or successfully parent our children. And yet, many multiples are functional, some highly so. Of course, some people with DID may have significant difficulties functioning in many areas of their lives—especially if they have not found a workable system of re-integration, or if they are not diligently working at healing from their trauma.

Some people, even one's own children, might seek to find ways to manipulate parts for their own purpose or agenda.

We may not want to believe someone close to us would do this, and not all persons will, but it is best to know this does happen sometimes.

There is a lot to think about and weigh, but this is not a decision which must happen immediately, so there is time to talk together, to journal, and to seek feedback from your therapist on their views.

Disclosure is a calculated risk, but it can often have positive results if done in healthy ways, in a healthy time-frame, and for the right reasons.

~~DID and Sexuality/Intimacy~~

This is a really hot topic—no pun intended. The mere mention of it is often met with dissociation and switching, subject-changing, averted eyes and defensive body-posturing, and sudden needs to visit the lavatory.

While not all trauma stems from or is related to physical or sexual abuse, enough does that issues related to sexuality and intimacy can be an incredibly difficult, though ultimately necessary topic to face and deal with.

Any time you are dealing with a sensitive topic, there is likely to be some degree of resistance. There may be many difficult challenges to navigate—triggers, fears, feelings of shame or disgust or self-consciousness. The reward of successfully facing and dealing with what is there is a lessening of what blocks the way to a richer, fuller, better life.

Between the twin topics of sexuality and intimacy, it is sometimes easier to talk about and deal with sexuality and sexual matters, than it is to deal with the matter of intimacy.

Intimacy is about opening one's self at deeper levels of trust and taking the risk of making one's self vulnerable to another—not only sexually, but emotionally as well. When there has been violation (physical, sexual, emotional, mental or spiritual), or when there has been betrayal, true intimacy can feel very frightening, even threatening.

If you have disclosed your multiplicity to your spouse or partner, good, honest, timely communication will be a must in keeping the relationship healthy and strong.

It's important to not just communicate honestly, but as your relationship grows or as it deepens over time, it is important to not keep secrets from each other.

If you are in a sexual relationship with another person, it is important to establish healthy bounds so everyone in the System feels safe.

One part may have no triggers or traumas about sex and may wish to enjoy the activity. Another alter may have been sexually violated, and therefore unable to participate in or even witness this. There are ways of taking care of this part so there is not further upset. They can find a way of shielding themselves in the Dome during this limited time, or they could perhaps go to a space in the Dome where the monitors and speakers can be turned off for a while, so they are not triggered, in fear, or in distress. Perhaps they can 'buddy up' with another part to talk about what is going on for them, or simply for some comforting and reassurance.

An equally important thing is for your partner to feel safe.

It will be important to set a time—outside of times of sexual activity—to sit down and allow the partner to think about and map out what it is they need to feel safe and comfortable in sexually intimate settings. The System needs to do the same thing. (The same principle can apply to other areas of the relationship—division of household chores, parenting, relating to others in outside settings as a couple, etc.) It might even be helpful to take time to write these things down. Then talk about what needs to happen so that not just the System feels safe, but that your partner does as well. That is going to be essential for the relationship—in all of it's facets—to be healthy, strong, and mutually satisfying, fulfilling, and respectful.

It will be important for everyone's sake, and for the sake of the relationship, to have arrangements known and agreed upon beforehand with the partner, as to which part in the System will engage in the sexual activity. Some Systems and their partners are comfortable with more than one part participating in the sexual activity, some are not. Some partners may need assurances or an agreement from the System that others who are not participating sexually are not 'watching' or 'being an audience' through the monitors and speakers in the Dome.

Relationships, including sexual ones, are multi-layered and often filled with subtle complexities and shadings.

Regarding sex and relationships, one insightful System had this to say:

> "We look for what we know. Sadly, people who grow up abused look for others to continue the abuse. It's comfortable and as a child, the abuse is taken into the love concept. 'I do this because I love you' has been a statement many have heard in one form or another and over the years, we believe it and incorporate it in our relationships. Unfortunately, there have been times where I've incorporated my partner into my abuse needs whether they liked it or not. For example, rough sex, instigating quarrels or conflict, etc. Mostly, we find someone who meets this need without much help from ourselves. Often, we will abuse ourselves as well to keep the mental balance in our head."

This System went on to write:

> "I think sex has been an addictive and complicated role for me to be involved in. If a DID person is forced, hatred will grow. If they feel unable to say 'no' or 'I'd rather not,' a code or a gesture could be established between two people that would let the partner know it is triggering at this time and try later. For myself, I was forced so many times; I tried to find a way to accept what was happening without being hurt. I tried to find a way to tune out and enjoy it on some level. I was successful but hated him for it. I honestly don't have any problems having sex at this time. However, it does take me a long time to become comfortable with someone where I feel free to give my body."

Unhealthy Sexual Expressions

Unhealthy sexual expressions are sometimes about power or control over another. Sometimes they are expressions of the need to 'prove' one's self and/or one's sexual prowess or sexual attractiveness. Sometimes the unhealthiness is a matter of selfish disregard of one's partner, and engineering the sexual activity or experience to cater to one's own pleasure or gratification with disregard to one's partner.

Unhealthy sexual expression can include, among other things, masochism, sadomasochism/bondage, fetishism, voyeurism/exhibitionism, sexual addictions, promiscuity, prostitution (solicitation of a prostitute or performing as a prostitute), viewing or participating in pornography, etc.

Unhealthy sexual expression can also include marital rape, and/or forcing or coercing or intimidating your partner into doing anything they do not want to do, or with which they are not comfortable. It also includes calling out particular parts who are sexually adept or sexually uninhibited, or manipulating or exploiting parts within Systems for the other person's pleasure or gratification.

Some people use rough or demeaning sex (or withholding sex) as a punishment. (They sometimes withhold cuddling, attention, compliments, and other forms of affection for the same reason.) While this is hurtful for a lot of people, the hurt can be magnified and devastating for someone who is DID.

Frigidity or impotence can sometimes arise as psychological and/or physical aftereffects of sexual abuse or torture. Because of abuse, some parts may only feel safe enough be able to reach orgasm by self-stimulation; others perhaps only reach orgasm by the infliction of pain, bondage, violence, humiliation, etc. (re-creating the original abuse). Some medications, including some anti-depressants and other psych meds, can affect libido. At some point, it may be important to check with a physician to see if there is a physical or medical condition causing these problems—and in that event, it will be important to share your diagnosis of DID, and your trauma history, so they can use this information in their evaluation, and in medical assessment of your overall health.

Masturbation (or as one System chooses to call it—PSI—Personal Self Intimacy) can be a legitimate and healthy form of sexual expression if done privately, and without pressure to do it for the express purpose of another's gratification, and simply for one's own pleasure and enjoyment or release.

Just like non-DID folks, different parts within a System may have a wide variety of sexual needs, desires, and challenges. Just as the System must get to know itself well, the partner must get to know the System, too. It can take patience and time to learn and explore what is there, in all of its variety, both for the System and for the partner. It's critical to emphasize that this is not something that can be rushed. The crucial elements in all of this—both within the System and between System and partner—are safety and respect, and honest, timely, compassionate communication—listening and sharing.

If you and your partner have an agreement that more than one part in your System is being sexual or intimate—just because the partner knows what pleases or frightens one part, they need to understand that that same information does not necessarily translate to any other part in the System.

This is not just true with sex, but with other things as well.

You are all different, so getting to know likes, dislikes, triggers, needs—everything...becomes quite complex. Good communication can aid here.

The good news is...getting to know the System's parts, in all of their unique forms and expressions, is a process which can bring delight and depth to the relationship that is unique to loving and caring for someone who is DID. This is true of any relationship the person with DID is in, not just the sexual ones.

Keeping the littles safe

What about sex...when you have littles in the System? This is a delicate, though very important question.

It is very important to have contracts and safety measures in place so there is no switching during sexual activity with a partner, and that littles do not come out and get scared or triggered. This is important not just for all in the System, but also for your sexual partner as well.

Though all of you in the System—young parts and older parts—have to co-exist within the same physical body, it is inappropriate and psychologically deleterious for a young part to be present during times when an adult part is engaging in sexual activity. Though the physical body may be of consenting age—twenty-one, thirty or fifty-eight—if an alter who is three or eight or twelve comes out... they *are*... three or eight or twelve, regardless of the age of the body they exist in... and that's a real problem that can't be allowed to happen.

Healthy sexual expression is a solid and worthwhile goal. Sex is a normal and natural part of life which sexual and physical (and sometimes emotional) abuse (past or present) may have corrupted. We are sexual beings, along with everything else we are. There is nothing wrong with working to reclaim that which may have been stolen or tainted through the actions of others. Healthy sexual expression, conveyed through thoughtful, respectful affection and mutually agreed upon acts of intimacy, both with one's self and with others, can enhance and bring joy and contentment to life.

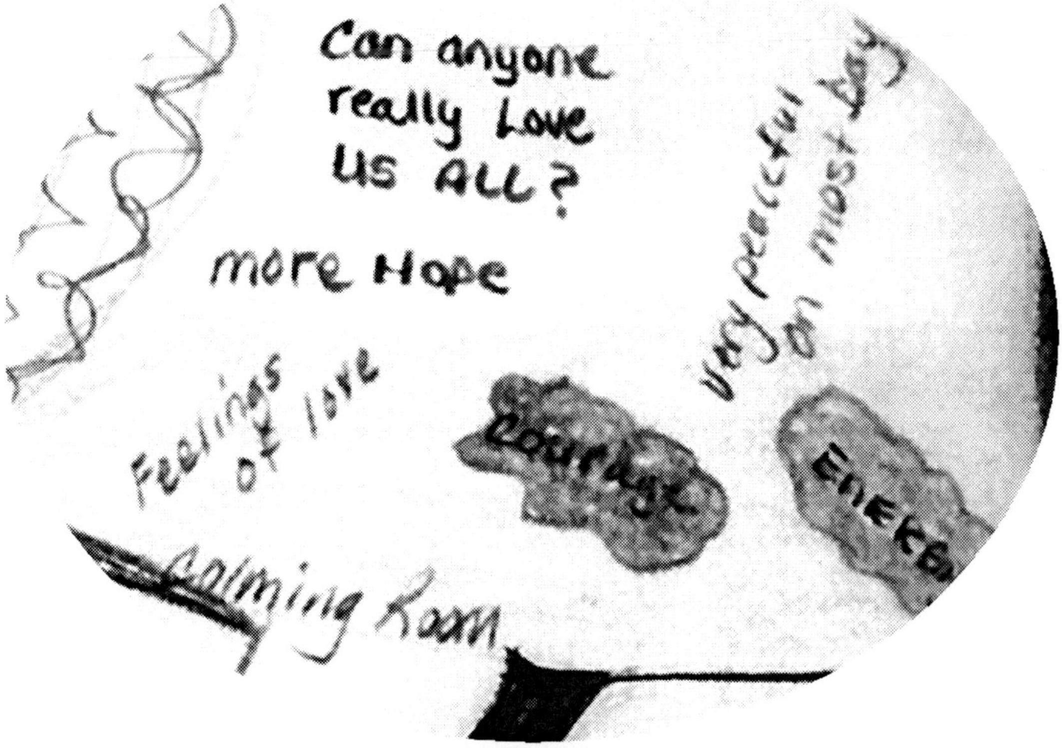

~~DID and Relationships~~

None of us live in a vacuum, or in complete isolation from outside others. There is 'family'—either your family of origin, or your adoptive family, or the family you have created with a mate. Sometimes people create a new, safe, 'family of choice' of friends and others to whom they are not biologically or genetically related. There are our 'significant others' (spouse, partner, lover). There are friends; business relationships/colleagues; social acquaintances; and those we date, among others.

Not to be forgotten are the pets in our lives—those, too, are important relationships we have. The unconditional love and affection and devotion of pets are sometimes overlooked or minimized for their healing effect. Scientific studies have shown having a pet lowers blood pressure, increases feelings of self-confidence and self-worth, and fights against the effects of loneliness and depression.

It surprises many with DID to discover that others already know we are multiple. Many people in our lives already either know, or have some sense of our multiplicity, though they may not know what it's called, or know much about it. It often makes sense to them, because it accounts for things they have been seeing and hearing—sometimes for years—without having anything to explain or back up their observations and experiences.

A common question is "How do you know if/when to disclose your DID (multiplicity) to another?" This is a somewhat gray and misty area. Unfortunately, there is no exact, right, absolute answer. (The main person(s) where there is no gray area on whether to disclose are your health care providers.) There are some additional observations and insights on disclosure in *Disclosure* on page 54, and in the section on Parenting on page 69.

Some general guidelines to use as a kind of 'litmus test' might be to ask yourself: is this person normally loving, caring, supportive, and accepting of me in all areas of my life, regardless of how I seem to be doing? Do I see or hear this person making offensive or disrespectful remarks about people with handicaps/mental illness/disabilities? What might the relationship gain or lose by my disclosure? What is my reason for wanting to disclose to this particular person? It's a good idea to write down your answers as you are talking amongst yourselves about this.

Ask yourselves, what if we receive a negative or hurtful response to our disclosure? Would we be able to handle it, or would it send us reeling off into self-harming or self-destructive behaviors until or unless we could sort our feelings and thoughts out with the help of our therapist?

If you are seriously thinking about disclosing to your spouse or partner, consider this. They likely will know you are in therapy anyway, so that may be a natural opening, and a more safe-feeling way to do your disclosing—by having a joint session with you, your partner, and your therapist.

There are no absolute guarantees when you are disclosing. This is something you need to know ahead of time. Still, disclosing to the right people—persons you have close and already established relationships with, as opposed to casual friendships or business or work relationships with—at the right time, for the right reasons, can have very good outcomes.

Close interpersonal relationships can be challenging for a lot of people.

When you are DID, the challenge to have healthy, safe, mutually satisfying relationships is greatly increased, and there are different types of challenges. There are often issues of trust, betrayal, abandonment, triggers, having been physically, sexually, mentally, emotionally, or spiritually abused or neglected...

The reverse is true here, too—

Having a family member, spouse/partner, or friend who is DID can be frightening, difficult, stressful, and very confusing. It can be achingly sad to come to realize the person for whom you feel such closeness or affection has been so grievously, traumatically wounded that trauma has resulted in fragmenting of self into multiple selves. Those close to us may be unwitting witness to our nightmares, night terrors, triggers, flashbacks, or devastatingly painful body memories. This can take a real toll on the relationship.

Some parts may be open and trusting, easy-going, playful. Other parts may be easily frightened, have an exaggerated startle response, or be easily and frequently triggered. Some parts may be distant, or unable to trust, or may dissociate easily. Some parts may be outright hostile. This variety within what 'looks like the same person' or 'seems like the same person' to others (until or unless they know about our multiplicity, and/or get to know the System) can be strange and hard to be around.

It naturally follows that often, the amount of distress and chaos the System's Inner World is experiencing reflects back out into the outer world of relationship-with-others, and can bring with it the unpredictable, chaotic, short-emotionally-fused, confused and confusing disintegration of all that is going on inside the System.

In counterpoint, as parts heal from their traumas, and the System moves toward ever-greater re-integration, their ever-more-healing and ever-more balanced state is reflected back out to others, as well.

While it can be incredibly enriching and rewarding to know and be in relationship with someone who is DID, it also requires exercising compassion and great patience, calling out your best communication skills, being flexible and supportive, and having a strong sense of humor. It is also essential you maintain your own healthy boundaries, and critical you do your own good self care.

Regardless of the pain or distress the person you are in relationship with is in, it is not all about them, or only about them. You are a just-as-important person in the relationship, and you do not have to give up living your life to cater to what it is they need at any particular place in their healing and re-integration process.

It is important to find that delicate balance between genuinely demonstrating you are caring for this person, and becoming emotionally enmeshed in their pain and struggle. That balance is not easily found, but it is a critical goal for you to find your own place here. Here again, good communication skills come into play, as your DID friend or loved one may not always understand—at least in the beginning—when at times it may seem at times like you are being distant, or pulling away. It is important for you to make sure you have your own outside interests, friendships and support networks.

Most people with DID do not intend to be overwhelming with their upset and 'neediness'—and realize that everyone has needs—needs aren't necessarily bad, nor unhealthy to have—it's just that the expression or frequency those needs takes may not sometimes be healthy, that's all. Many folks with DID do not always recognize when their 'needs' or their 'issues' are negatively impacting or causing problems in a friendship or relationship. That's another area where good, timely, compassionate communication can help, though this won't be a panacea.

As the DID person continues to do their work to heal and re-integrate, this will naturally, if sometimes slowly, lessen the problems within their relationships.

Sometimes a joint session between you, the person with DID, and the DID person's therapist can be helpful in confronting and working through critical areas that are difficult to talk about. Often, the person with DID finds it hard to hear and understand what is being said. These struggles and impairments to understanding are neither deliberate nor intentional on the part of the person with DID; some of their origins may lie in a person's dysfunctional upbringing, or seeded in an unresolved adult trauma.

There are interesting ramifications concerning a major commitment like marriage. One part got married. Sometimes, another part is 'out' around the spouse, and this one has not entered into a marriage, and yet has an important relationship with the spouse. All the parts do. That can sometimes create a raft of unforeseen problems and chaos under the right (or wrong) conditions—especially if the other person does not know you are DID.

One System had this to say:

> "For someone with DID, any relationship is a challenge. Choosing someone to spend your life with and who will accept you for who you are and what has happened to you presents the greatest challenge. In my System there are about fifteen parts. Now ask yourself what it would be like to have a partner that can change from loving to angry in the blink of an eye or from happy to despondent and sad. For that partner to change not only in moods but also mannerisms and in all aspects become someone else. To find a partner who can not only accept this and to agree to be part of it but to continue to love you in all the ups and downs is challenging.

"Think about all the people in your life. Can you think of one person that fifteen different people would agree upon to spend the rest of their lives with as a partner ? This is a problem a DID person faces. Say ten out of the fifteen parts agree on someone. That leaves five parts that will work to destroy that relationship."

People enter into marriages and relationships for all sorts of reasons.

Regarding the 'whys' and needs of entering into relationships, one System wrote:

> Save yourself—Don't expect to find a partner to 'save' you. We have to do the work to save ourselves. As we are often stuck in the past as children, a common hope is for someone to come along and scoop us up to save us since as children we didn't have the ability to save ourselves. This sets us up for disappointment and failure because no one can save us but ourselves. Our therapist should guide and support us to find the tools to become strong, independent people that may enjoy sharing our life with someone who is a friend, lover and support as we can learn to be one to someone else."

Another System made these observations

> "I guess the biggest part of making a relationship work is really getting to know a person and find out how they feel about things and do a lot of talking and ask a lot of questions. If you are afraid to ask then that person doesn't make you comfortable and maybe you should take a much better look at who they are and why they make you feel this way."

I think most DID people rush into relationships because they fear rejection. Like if they really get the chance to know me they will leave or because they feel this person is the best they deserve and they should be grateful that they even want them. When you go through the trauma of abuse and that abuser tells you over and over how little you are worth and no one will ever love you, you learn to believe what they say. So when you become an adult and begin looking for someone to love you in the back of your head is always those words. You perceive yourself as unlovable so when someone actually acts like they love you, no matter how much that love hurts, you cling to it with all you have and accept it as the only love you are worth receiving."

When you are DID and are in a relationship with someone, it is critical for you to continue to do your own individual work to heal from your trauma, and the System-work necessary for re-integration (including contracts and System meetings), if you want the relationship you are in to work and to be successful.

It is important for the System to discuss inside their feelings, thoughts, and opinions—about things in general, but also about the other person in the relationship whether it is a spouse/partner, friend, business colleague or whomever.

If a part is refusing to provide any feedback or input about something, by rights, they lose some of their say and some of their right to complain about any outcomes or results that come from System discussions regarding the relationship (or about an endeavor).

Though it can be at times potentially scary, uncomfortable, or awkward, it is most generally a good idea for every part to at least have a talking relationship with their spouse/partner. The same can be extended to a close friendship, if the relationship is especially close and you have disclosed your multiplicity to your friend. Though sometimes challenging, it can open these relationships to newer, closer, deeper levels which can be rewarding for both parties.

Also, as the other person in the relationship comes to know you ever-better, at least ideally, they can come to understand what angers, frightens, upsets, or disorients individual ones of you, and help be a support and help you find ways of coming through these challenges.

For example, if a teen-age part is acting out because of anger or loneliness, a partner who cares about the System and has gotten to know that part—even a little, though they are not a therapist, they may be able to confront and talk to that part in a way that can get through to them perhaps even differently than another part inside might be able to.

It can be an amazing feeling to have someone communicate in ways spoken or unspoken—"I care about all of you, I want to work on making this relationship even better, I want to help (this person/s) whom I have grown to care about."

Unhealthy relationships are damaging, destructive, demeaning, and draining.

Unhealthy relationships tend to have issues of control, and often tend to be more unbalanced over time (the give and take of the relationship something grossly disproportional, like 80-20, or 20-80, and staying in that proportion for extended periods of time, with less of the healthy moving back and forth of give and take).

Unhealthy relationships are often based on unhealthy or unrealistic expectations of what the other person 'should' be or of what the relationship 'should' be. They are also based in unhealthy definition and understanding of 'power'. This is not just about 'power over' another, but also includes 'giving away your own power' to someone else. In unhealthy relationships, there is often a disproportionately exaggerated or de-valued sense of 'self' and 'self's needs' (for either or both people). The unhealthiness in relationships sometimes coalesces around frozen or static ideas, and often around unresolved and unhealed past issues (for either or both people).

Unhealthy relationships thrive in an atmosphere of fear and silence.

Another example of unhealthiness in relationships with those who are DID is calling out parts for selfish purpose, or manipulating parts in someone's System.

Parts do not exist for someone else's use or convenience. Parts are not there to be called out for someone's amusement like they are 'the Amazing-Switching-DID-Girl' at the sideshow. Do not request another part to come out simply because they are 'more fun', or 'you'd rather be around them than another part'. That is very, very hurtful. It is reckless and incredibly damaging to call out parts merely because 'they're cute' (like littles), or because 'they're unbelievable in bed', or because they are an immaculate housekeeper.

Parts are not 'pets' to be used, played with, and discarded...we are real, and we have feelings. Along these lines, one System cautions:

> "I've been in semi-relationships where the partner knew most all of my parts and wanted to call certain personalities out for various tasks, mostly sex. This is hurtful to the person who is out, and feels manipulative. For some, it may be ok to ask if so and so is available, but these details would need to be worked out on a person to person basis. If someone is in a relationship and wants to be a participant, it's important they don't say that they like one part more than another and allow their partner to have the room to express these different sides. Some may need some time to be alone. Some may want to color. The partner could choose to color as well or sit on the floor and chat to bond with that part."

Healthy relationships are based on several basic, but essential premises—mutuality, respect, reciprocity, and valuing the other individual(s). Healthy relationships are fluid, flexible, dynamic, and mutually enriching and mutually satisfying.

All relationships involve sharing, and a back and forth mix of give and take. Within good, working relationships, the give and take is seldom exactly 50%-50%. It's usually more like 60-40, or 40-60, or 52-48, or 30-70, or 75-25. The proportional balance swings with the natural rhythm of give and take that is present in all relationships.

Healthy relationships will change over time, because the persons within those relationships are changing, growing, learning and maturing. If relationships do not change, they can stagnate and draw both partners into a less healthy place, and a place where all are left less than and other than they could be otherwise.

The partner of one System made this great analogy of being in relationship with someone who is DID. They described it like a wonderful and delicious stew—all the individual ingredients which go into the stew are good and tasty in and of themselves, but when they are combined, and allowed to simmer and mix and complement each other—at an indescribable point they combine to create a unique dish that would not be the same if any one ingredient had not been there.

If you are not currently in a relationship, but hope to be one day, one System offers this advice:

"Analyze yourself and your needs. I know it won't be perfect but write down your likes and dislikes. Make a list of the things you think you need from a partner.

Then look for that. Don't expect to find someone who meets all your needs but someone who can take care of the big ones. No one person can meet all of someone's needs. You will need to find some needs met with other relationships, like friends or family. This is healthy and should be done by both partners. Allow each other to do this."

Another System writes:

My advice to any DID person is as follows...

1. Take time to find out what real love is and what it means.

2. Learn to love yourself.

3. Accept nothing but true love (love doesn't equal sex).

4. Learn to relax and accept kindness. Not everyone is after something!

5. Know the person you are trusting. Make sure they deserve trust.

6. Have meetings deal with conflicts when they arise, not weeks later.

7. Be as good to yourself as you are to others.

~~DID and Parenting~~

First, a critical note:

If you are, or even suspect you may be, abusive to your children... get your children and yourself immediate professional help and intervention.

Being DID is never an excuse to abuse, mistreat or neglect your children.

Being a parent is a stressful, challenging, demanding, full time job.

Being a parent, *and* being DID presents even more challenges and stresses. Unfortunately there is no rule book or guide book for this. However, there are some things that can be helpful to know.

First of all, it can be done.

It is possible to be DID, *and* to do the work to recover from the trauma that caused the splitting in the first place, to continue the re-integration work that is necessary for a fuller, healthier, more functional and peaceful life *and* to be a good parent. Others have found ways to balance this, and it is possible for you to also.

One of the best things you can do is to dial up your own self care and make sure you are taking the absolute best care of yourself you-all are capable of doing.

As hard as it might be to make time, and take time for yourself—for taking care of yourself, for doing your therapy work, for relaxation and things which bring enjoyment, it is something that will help you to eventually, if not right away, have more reserves of energy and patience for dealing with the challenges of parenting.

In the fuller picture of things, anything you-all can do to do your own recovery work, to re-integrate, and get yourselves healthier is taking care of your children because it is not only giving them a healthier mom or dad better able to parent them, but it is also modeling behaviors the kids themselves will be able to learn from and use in their own lives.

As in other areas of life, it might be helpful, at least until the System has stabilized some and is working more in concert and has a higher degree of cooperation and co-consciousness, to agree to have only certain parts be out around and dealing with your children.

There is often a part or parts in a System who deals better with children, relates to them better, has more patience, more and healthier parenting skills than do some other parts. Let those who are better at this...do it. If an alter part (or parts) does not like kids, or regards them as a never-ending source of frustration and anger, or if they have significant unresolved trauma around their own childhood or their relationship with their parent growing up, those are good cues to leave the parenting of your own children to some other part. It will be better for you, and better for your kids.

This strategy can cut down on some of the personality switches and shifts that might be confusing or even frightening to the children.

It might be worth working on developing better parenting skills throughout the System, but the immediate focus is to take good care of yourselves and to take good care of your children.

Kids are very bright, and while they may not say anything, if they sometimes see different alters, they will likely recognize something is different, even if they cannot put a name or explanation to it. This isn't necessarily a bad thing, it just is.

Though kids are very perceptive, and may suspect there is something 'different' about mom or dad, if the System can make a generally unified presentation to the children, it will go a long way in making them feel more stable and more secure and ok in themselves and in their home-life and family interactions.

The question will likely come up at some point whether or not to disclose your DID (multiplicity) to your children. This is a very individual area, and a very personal decision. There is no absolute right or wrong answer.

If it seems appropriate, or if it might be reassuring or helpful, there are ways of disclosing your multiplicity in healthy, gentle, age-appropriate ways that can help children to understand and make a better sense of things.

Part of the decision-making process will involve taking into account the children's ages and maturity level, the children's own emotional health and adjustment, and kind and strength of the children's support system.

Another part of the decision whether to disclose would be to consider what would be gained by telling or not telling.

You should also consider if there is a likelihood your child might overhear, or see something in writing that will disclose your status as DID. You may believe this is something over which you have control, but it is impossible to be absolutely in control of your external environment, and of what the people in your life may say.

In the event of your child unwittingly learning about your DID, there might be hurt, anger, or feelings of confusion or betrayal. There might possibly even be fear—that DID is something worse or something other than what it is—and that is why you did not tell them yourself.

What-ifs cannot be your entire reason for disclosing or not disclosing your diagnosis to your child, and you do not automatically 'owe' your child this information. While deliberately keeping your DID 'close to the vest' might or might not be seen as perpetuating secrets, sometimes our actions can catch up with us later in ways hard to predict.

This is a scenario you might want to role-play with your therapist, just in case you get caught unawares.

If you choose to disclose, here is something to think about. See whether you can remain matter-of-fact, and not focus on the drama (or melodrama) of DID. This can help children to see multiplicity as a creative coping mechanism rather than a mysterious, frightening mental illness or mental defect. You will help to de-mystify DID and perhaps allay unspoken fears mom or dad might not be able to take care of them or that they may become DID themselves.

After you have disclosed your DID, and provided limited, matter-of-fact and age-appropriate information about DID and why it occurs, some kids will immediately have a sense of relief that what they have been seeing or sensing finally makes sense.

Still, it's possible that other kids might become frightened or withdrawn or have other reactions which might be difficult for you to deal with. If you are having difficulty dealing with your child's reaction to your disclosure, enlist the help of your therapist.

Be prepared that kids will likely, at one point or another, have their own questions about DID and 'what's wrong' with mom or dad. Do not feel you have to reveal everything about your trauma history, or 'war stories' about what it is like to be DID.

The more poised and matter-of-fact you can remain in answering their questions, the better it will be in showing to your children DID is not a horrible affliction, but rather a creative coping skill that helped you live through something very traumatic.

Whether you like it or not, whether you want to admit it or not, your trauma history and the resulting DID will more than likely be impacting your children in at least some way and to some degree. This does not in and of itself make you a bad person, or a bad parent. It can be increased motivation to continue to do your own work to heal and to re-integrate.

Your therapist can talk with you about ways in which talking to your kids about DID can be accomplished, and how and when and where to seek help for the kids, should they need support themselves.

Don't let this frighten you off—just keep taking good care of yourselves, and of your children, and if and when the time or opportunity is right, then you can explore your options.

All of this work is a learning process, and all you can do is keep trying your best. Keep doing good self care, have daily meetings, keep talking and working together inside and communicating with your therapist, and keep doing the work.

Keep learning as you go, tracking what works, what doesn't, and what might work if done a bit differently. These will be your saving graces throughout all of this.

~~DID and Working/Employment~~

It can sometimes be difficult and challenging to work when you are DID, especially if you-all are early on your healing and re-integration path.

Many Systems have found that, as it is in other areas in life, it is often helpful to designate a part or (very limited) number of parts that are the going-to-work parts or the 'work team'.

These parts would be the ones best skilled, best suited physically, emotionally, and mentally to deal with being in a particular work environment. This would be the only part (or parts) that would actually go to work and be in the work environment, the only ones who would interact with those in the workplace or with customers, clients, etc, and the only ones to perform the actual work.

If the rest of the System is utilizing the monitors and speakers well, and has learned to work and cooperate together, they can view the work scene and what goes on to gain information and to become more conscious as to what happens there and be supportive of the work team.

It's most often best for those who are not on the work team to have agreements or contracts to not come out at work and to let the part who is there do their job without interference or without switching that has not been previously agreed on.

Having a plan in place—and following the plan, adjusting it as necessary—can often reduce the chaos, confusion, and problems that can arise both inside and outside.

It may be that, at a particular stage of trauma recovery and re-integration, the System as a whole is unable to find ways to function in a work setting. It may be impossible to find parts who are able to work.

Try to not be hard on yourselves for being where you are in this process—this healing and re-integration work is incredibly difficult sometimes. You may be able to find ways of surviving financially while not working, or reducing the number of working hours, or finding ways of reducing job stressors. Explore such options.

As you continue to heal from the trauma you-all experienced, and as you continue to do the work to re-integrate and to manage your life ever-better as DID, you will likely find you are able to reintroduce things, or add things back to your life you were not able to do before.

The Americans with Disabilities Act (ADA) concerns issues such as disclosure, what protection the law offers, job accommodations, discrimination concerns, and such. This information can be found at the library or at http://www.ada.gov/. Finding out more about the ADA is a good place to start learning how to integrate what DID challenges you may experience in your workplace setting within what the law allows, so you are afforded the best opportunity for success in your work.

Your local office of Vocational Rehabilitation, or Veteran's Center are other places where you can receive information/assistance in disability/employment related matters.

~~DID and School~~

The same strategy used in the workplace can be applied if you are at school, whether full time or part time, elementary or middle grades, high school, college, or graduate studies.

It is generally helpful to designate a particular part or parts (or have parts volunteer) to handle everything related to school—to attend classes, take notes, do lab work, do homework, take tests, and so on, whatever is required. Usually there is someone inside who has some interest in or talent for the subjects, or at least has the ability to stay focused and applied (sometimes difficult when you are multiple), in order to get the most out of classes and school.

The part who agrees to attend school and to do the school-work must take responsibility to follow through and do the best they are able. If, after giving it a fair chance, though not so late in the year that there are grave problems, they find they are unable to handle the class or do the work, then the System, possibly with your therapist's help, can come up with an alternative plan.

The rest of the System needs to help by not interfering with the 'school team' unless the school part specifically requests occasional, specific assistance, and then only in limited ways out of the class/library/study environment. This way, there will be less chance of switching and chaos and someone ending up in class and being totally unprepared, overloaded and out of their element. None of you need more surprise or chaos or preventable stress in your lives.

Many schools have provisions for, and are in some cases able to make certain accommodations for students with disabilities/special needs. There is nothing wrong with needing assistance, and there is nothing to be ashamed about in articulating your needs. Your local office of Vocational Rehabilitation is another resource where you can find help in the areas of disability/schooling.

7 Guidelines for Living

~~This May Not Be Something You Want To Hear Or Believe, But...~~

Continuing to recover memories and discovering parts you haven't known about may continue for awhile. Don't be dismayed or disheartened. This doesn't mean you are getting 'worse'. It's just a part of the process of discovery and recovery, and the tide does abate after a time. This never totally goes away; this never really ends. You will always be a survivor of trauma. You cannot turn back time and make it not have happened. Trauma can, however, be worked through with diligence and courage, come to terms with, and ultimately moved beyond.

You will always be DID. DID is managed, it is not 'cured'. Parts sometimes go into hiding, or seem dormant, especially if they are being abused or neglected by others in the System, or if the System is not working and cooperating together; parts do not go away, and they do not die. The DID/multiplicity challenge can be managed with solid System work and attention to the efforts necessary to re-integrate. Still, the work does not end there. It is important to realize recovery and re-integration are not static events, but rather ongoing journeys. Healing is a continuum, and moving forward with your life is an ongoing, ever-evolving process.

There will always be work to do. The on-going work may not always be as intense or grueling, but challenges will continue to come up, usually when you least expect them. That's why it is critical to keep up with daily meetings and self care and whatever it takes to keep the System 'happy, healthy and humming along,' and to do it mindfully, in a serious, conscientious, and timely manner. There is no time or place for sulking, bickering, pettiness, for ego trips or games, for denial, or for thinking you're all 'fixed' and don't need to keep up with this exacting work.

Although we have tried to take a light-hearted tone in this book, doing this daily ongoing work is an absolutely serious matter. It is, literally, a matter of *life and death*. It does get better, and it is possible to have a good, satisfying, productive life, but it takes hard work, and acknowledging you-all are in this for the long haul.

~~Important Questions~~

Four Important Questions for Systems to ask of themselves as situations arise:

1. Who's here?
2. What's going on for you?
3. What do you need right now?
4. Are you the most appropriate part to be here right now?

Another Important Question to ask:

Is what I am doing right now helping my own healing to progress, and is it contributing to the over-all health and progress of the System-as-a-whole?

A helpful, enlightening exercise:

When you are complaining or frustrated or stuck or worried or fretful or fearful...

Write down a list of twenty-five things that *are more important* than whatever is going on right now that has you in this upset state.

Guideposts

Four Guideposts to look to when you are struggling:

1. Focus: One thing at a time—what's right in front of you, what's the most important thing you need to remember, pay attention to, or do right now?

2. Grounding: Find a way to center, stabilize, anchor yourself so you are not aimlessly adrift or caught in the undertow of what is going on right now.

3. Energy Conservation: You only have a certain amount of physical, mental and emotional energy to spend on any one thing at any one time—it's important to make wise and efficient use of that energy. Ask, is this the best use of my energy right now?

4. Direction: Are you sure what you are doing is taking you in the direction you truly wish to go? If not, remember you can choose to change direction and make different choices at any time.

~~The Power of Belief / The Power of the Spoken Word~~

There was a famous philosopher, who, having a difficult time reconciling himself to life's disappointments, unfairness, pain, capriciousness, heartache, heartbreak...decided to live his life 'as if'. 'As if' things mattered. 'As if' there was love out there. 'As if' there was meaning, and purpose to life. 'As if'.

A healthy exercise for all who struggle and see no meaning, no purpose, no hope—is to try the same thing. For a designated time, and make it longer than you anticipate thinking of doing it for—behave and speak and act 'as if'. *As if* life is not a horrible punishment. *As if* being multiple is not a curse. *As if* there is a reason you are here, and a purpose for your life. *As if* it is better to behave and speak in a positive way as opposed to a negative way. *As if* life will be better as you continue to do this work. *As if* you can get through this. Even if you don't necessarily believe these things now...go on and act and speak *as if they are true.*

In many ways, some that scientists (yes, scientists) are just beginning to understand, our thoughts, and what we say (both out loud or silently to ourselves) help to create a physical reality. This includes everything we say in conversations, or during the course of a day, things we mutter under our breath, affirmations, things we say in prayer—everything. Positive/good thoughts and words reinforce positive things. Negative reinforces negative.

There is the story of a certain Buddhist monk. He survived the Killing Fields of Cambodia during the brutal, oppressive Khmer Rouge regime, and had lived a torturous, nearly impossible life. He maintained a cheerful countenance, a positive outlook, and spent his life in joyful, selfless service to others. He was being interviewed by a journalist who was quite perplexed, and asked the monk how, despite all the horrific things he had witnessed, the things had been done to him, and what he had lived through—how he could remain so positive, so cheerful, so trusting and giving to others. The monk replied that when he was positive, he felt much better than when he was living, feeling, and behaving negatively, and he said (something to the effect)— "I like how I feel when I am positive."

Try the above experiment—really give it a wholehearted try—for a time long enough to see its effects—at least six months—and see if there are any differences you can notice. (Are you are feeling any better, and if there are any changes in how your life is going, and how you are doing in your day-to-day responses to life, and so on.)

~~Things to remember~~

You are good, you are important, you have value. You are not crazy, and you are not a freak. You have suffered great wounding—trauma others might not have survived at all. What you experienced did not make you bad, or any less of a person. What happened to you, what was done to you, what you may have been forced to do (even after you were older) was not your fault.

It's ok to live. It's ok to be happy. It's ok to have a good life. You are deserving of those things, and you always have been.

You are way ahead if you are lucky enough to have found a therapist trained in recognizing and treating trauma survivors, and who is adept at recognizing and accurately diagnosing Dissociative Identity Disorder, and who understands what is required to re-integrate alters and manage life successfully with this diagnosis.

It is really important to do the things your therapist asks you to do even if you don't understand the reason why at the time, even when it is inconvenient, hard, frightening, or wrenchingly painful to do so. There is a reason, and that's to work to heal from the trauma that caused the splitting, and to reclaim your power, so you can live the best life possible for you-all.

For that reason, also, it's important to be totally honest with your therapist. Therapists are canny, but they aren't mind readers. They can't help you with what they don't know about. When your trust has been betrayed before, it's hard to trust again, though it is important to work toward this.

You have to face what happened in your past before you can truly move on in your life. You can't run from it, and it doesn't go away. Doing this work allows you to move out of the past's sway, and into a future unbound from that past.

Trauma work often comes in layers. Sometimes you will work on a particular issue for a time and achieve some measure of understanding and resolution, only to find that same issue (or a similar one, or something that issue has stirred up) creeping back into your life at some point. This does not negate any of the hard work you have already done. This is simply an indication that traumatic events are complex and multi-layered, and sometimes require more attention—and in differing ways—as you continue to work through them over time to reclaim and rebuild your life.

It's ok to not have all the answers. It's ok to ask for help, and guidance, and information, and feedback, and ideas, and encouragement. It's ok to ask others to help you identify choices.

It's ok to have needs. It's ok to ask for what you need. Just realize those you ask may not always be able to meet those needs. That doesn't mean they don't care about you, and it doesn't mean you don't deserve to have those needs met, or you were wrong to ask. It's ok to keep searching out ways to get those needs met.

There may be times when you may begin to wonder, or doubt whether your traumatic experience ever happened, or if it was really 'that bad'. There may also be times when you may question, even go into denial about whether or not you really are DID. This is very normal. Journal about your thoughts and perceptions, ask questions and check things out—inside and out. Don't get stuck here, or let this derail you.

If you get stuck in 'analysis paralysis'—insisting on understanding everything, or knowing everything, or in having absolute 'proof' and verification of everything—you will lose untold time and precious energy. Sometimes it comes down to intuition, faith, trust...and deciding that even though you don't have all the answers, or don't know everything you long to know...you can still move on in reclaiming your life.

'Control' is a mirage, an illusion. The only things any of us can control are <u>our own</u> individual attitudes, speech, actions and behaviors.

There is a difference between doing something and *trying* to do something.

Healing, getting better, reclaiming your life *is* possible. The work to do this is messy, painful, inconvenient, grueling, and time-consuming. Yet, it beats the alternative. <u>And</u>, you are the only one who can do this work; no one can do it for you.

You *<u>do</u>* have choices. Do not mistake difficult or unpleasant choices with having no choices. Nobody ever said this would be easy.

Being DID is not an excuse to take no responsibility for one's actions and one's life.

This work *<u>is</u>* work, but it is not 100% pain and drudgery; there can be joyful, poignant, humorous and lighthearted moments as well.

There are worse things in this world, and in this life, than being DID.

Strive for *progress*, not perfection...

Don't hold your breath...*breathe*...

Remember... it's a process

and...

When you wonder, or are asked "how long does it take to recover from trauma, and to re-integrate?"...the answer is—

It takes as long as it takes.

In the world of trauma recovery and DID re-integration, there are no 'shoulds', 'normals', 'typicals', or 'expecteds', because everyone has a particular and unique experience.

Unless you truly are, for whatever reason—stalling, resisting, deflecting from, or simply making the intentional choice to not do the work, do not let others chastise you or shame you for not 'getting better quicker'. And try to refrain from doing this to yourself. It doesn't, and it won't, help.

Consistently doing the work (inside and outside) is what will assist you in getting to the place you want to be. This involves learning what works for you and your System and what does not work, learning to live and work well together as a System, and maintaining solid, regular, on-going self care. Just remember and keep reminding yourself/yourselves without self-judgment: it's a process, and it takes as long as it takes.

Two last, very important points to remember:

No two individuals, alters, Systems, historical experiences, etc. are ever identical. It is not fair to compare yourself, your System, your experiences, or your rate of progress with anyone else or with anyone else's System. Everyone's life and their trajectory of healing is different. Though sometimes tempting to do, comparing deflects away from what truly matters, and that is staying focused on your own issues and your own work.

and,

In the long run, the size of your System (the number of alter parts 'doesn't matter', in the sense the same basic rules apply, and the same steps need taken, whether you have four parts or forty or four hundred.

In the short run, however, those who have 'large' Systems (and that is a subjective term) will probably tell you that, to a degree, the time and energy required to have a cooperative, healing-through-time, and functional System, are proportional to the number of parts present.

Still, even 'large' Systems can do the work necessary to recover from trauma, and to re-integrate. You can get your life back and make it a good life, if it is what you-all desire—and if you are willing to work with grace and with humor, with time and with patience, with unflagging persistence, commitment, with hard, hard work, and working in concert together.

~~For Healing/For Re-integration/In Order to Create a Better Life...~~

You must believe it is possible to heal from your trauma, to live well despite having multiple personalities, and to live a fuller, better, more satisfying, (even happy) life.

- Make continual, conscious choices to heal.
- Be willing to do whatever it takes to heal.
- Strive to make ever-healthier choices and decisions, learn from mistakes and less-than-healthy decisions and choices, and do not beat yourself up for not being 'perfect' or 'there yet'.
- Each part must learn to love themselves.
- There must be no self-directed violence.
- All parts doing good thorough self care.
- All parts respecting, cooperating and working with each other.
- Parts must be able to trust each other.
- Each part must contribute all they are able.
- Each part must take personal responsibility for their words and action, for what they do and don't do; you-all must hold each other accountable for the same. The outside world regards us as one, and what one part says or does or does not do...affects the rest of you.
- Each part needs to process, in some form—talking, writing, some form of creative expression—their trauma experience and to express and share it in some way with others inside, with your therapist, in group.
- Each part needs to remember, to feel their feelings, to allow those feelings to come out, and to connect the feelings with the memories/experiences.
- Do the homework completely, honestly, and in a timely way.
- Use all tools available and continue to learn and gather new tools and skills.
- Be willing to take calculated risks, try new things, take leaps of faith.
- To heal you must be willing to sacrifice yourselves to the Truth.
- Don't ever give up...if there are missteps, mistakes, or setbacks, they do not have to de-rail you...remember you can choose to start right over again.

8 Helpful Resources

It will prove to be of great benefit to begin a running list of individual and System achievements and successes, along with the dates. This list can prove to be an extremely valuable reference when you are discouraged and feeling like you're not getting better or making any progress.

Another idea you might consider would be to get a blank notebook or journal in which to write inspirational quotes, poems, affirmations.

This notebook can also be used to write down compliments and positive feedback you-all have received.

You can also start your own list of books, tapes, websites, etc. you-all find especially helpful.

A Word about Outside Resources

The following pages contain lists of sources others have found helpful.

However, you may notice there are very few books or Internet sites here that specifically deal with, or are about, DID. There are a couple of reasons for that.

The first is likely to not be a popular stance; and it may not be something easy to accept or understand.

While it can be a real temptation to read everything you can get your hands on in your quest for information, for help, for answers—that may not be the best, healthiest thing. There can be inherent dangers in exposing yourself to too much information about DID. It's natural to want to understand more about this reality you-all find yourselves in. It's also important to balance your quest for information with realizing that there is much out there written about DID, both from professional, clinical perspectives, and by those who are DID themselves, much of which is off target, and some unhelpful.

While there is solid, helpful information out there, there is also a great deal in print, featured on television shows and news-magazine and talk shows, on the Internet, and in chat rooms—that other Systems have learned the hard way—contains material which can be misleading, triggering, even outright wrong, and can potentially be very hurtful to your process—at least until your System has stabilized, is working well together, and has done a portion of the re-integration work.

There are many theories about DID, about its validity as a psychological phenomenon, how DID (and it's attendant challenges) is best worked with, and many theories about integration/re-integration—sometimes contradictory, or controversial, often times upsetting.

It can be easy to keep reading, and read, and read, until you have read so much information—either technical/academic information, or personal accounts about being DID and living with DID, or both—that you can experience information overload.

This overload of theory, study, and anecdote can potentially put information (and more information) in front of you before you-all may be mentally and emotionally prepared for it. It can raise doubts and fears, and can cloud, even disrupt or sabotage the individual and group work you-all are doing with your own therapist.

At least in the beginning, your own System, and your therapist, are your best resources for understanding your own multiplicity.

Secondly, sadly, there are not as many resources out there as you might think, that contain accurate, factual, up-to-date, healthy and helpful information about and anecdotes relating to DID (either technical/clinical or personal accounts).

This is not to say sources other than those listed here do not exist, simply that Systems we know and interact with have not found many worth endorsing and passing along to others.

Books

Alderman, Tracy , and Karen Marshall. *Amongst Ourselves: A Self-Help Guide to Living with Dissociative Identity Disorder.* Oakland: New Harbinger, 1998.

Ban Breathnach, Sarah. *Simple Abundance: A Daybook of Comfort and Joy.* New York: Warner Books, 1995.

Ban Breathnach, Sarah. *The Simple Abundance Companion: Following Your Authentic Path to Something More.* New York: Warner, 2000.

Bass, Ellen, and Laura Davis. *The Courage to Heal: A Guide for Women Survivors of Child Sexual Abuse.* 3rd ed. New York: Harper & Row, 1988.

Beattie, Melody. *Codependent No More: How to Stop Controlling Others and Start Caring for Yourself.* Center City, MN: Hazelden, 1987.

Bloom, E. Sue. *Secret Survivors: Uncovering Incest and its Aftereffects in Women.* New York: Ballantine Books, a division of Random House, Inc., 1990.

Buscaglia, Leo F. *Born for Love: Reflections on Loving.* Thorofare, NJ: SLACK Inc. : Distributed by Random House, 1992.

Buscaglia, Leo F. *Personhood: The Art of Being Fully Human.* Thorofare: C. B. Slack ; New York : Distributed by Holt, Rinehart and Winston , 1978.

Capacchione, Lucia. *The Power of Your Other Hand: A Course in Channeling the Inner Wisdom of the Right Brain.* Rev. ed. Franklin Lakes, NJ: New Page Books, 2001.

Chopra, M.D., Deepak. *Quantum Healing: Exploring the Frontiers of Mind/Body Medicine.* New York: A Bantam Book, published by Bantam Books, a division of Bantam Doubleday Dell Publishing Group, Inc., 1989.

Crum, Thomas F. *Journey to Center: Lessons in Unifying Body, Mind, and Spirit.* New York: Simon & Schuster, 1997.

Crum, Thomas F. *The Magic of Conflict: Turning a Life of Work into a Work of Art.* New York: Simon & Schuster, 1987.

Davis, Laura. *The Courage to Heal Workbook: For Women and Men Survivors of Child Sexual Abuse.* New York: Harper & Row, 1990.

De Becker, Gavin. *The Gift of Fear: Survival Signals That Protect Us From Violence*. Boston: Little, Brown and Company, 1997.

Haddock, M.Ed., M.A., L.P., Deborah Bray. *The Dissociative Identity Disorder Sourcebook*. Chicago: Contemporary Books, A Division of the McGraw-Hill Companies, 2001.

Ingerman, Sandra. *Soul Retrieval: Mending the Fragmented Self*. San Francisco: Harper, 1991.

Kidd, Sue Monk. *The Secret Life of Bees*. New York: Viking Penguin, a member of Penguin Putnam, Inc., 2002.

Lew, Mike. *Victims No Longer: Men Recovering from Incest and Other Sexual Child Abuse*. New York: Perennial Library, 1990.

Mandino, Og. *The Greatest Miracle in the World*. New York: A Bantam Book, published by Bantam Books, Inc., published by arrangement with Frederick Fell Publishers, Inc., 1975.

Millman, Dan. *The Laws of Spirit: Simple, Powerful Truths for Making Life Work*. Tiburon, CA: HJ Kramer, Inc., 1995.

Millman, Dan. *Way of the Peaceful Warrior: A Book that Changes Lives.* Tiburon: H.J. Kramer, Inc., 1980.

Mundis, Jerrold. *How to Get Out of Debt, Stay Out of Debt, & Live Prosperously*. New York: A Bantam Book, published by Bantam Books, a division of Bantam Doubleday Dell Publishing Group, Inc., 1988.

Nhat Hanh, Thich. *The Blooming of a Lotus: Guided Meditation Exercises for Healing and Transformation*. Boston: Beacon Press, 1993.

Paulus, Trina. *Hope for the Flowers: A Tale—Partly about Life Partly about Revolution and Lots about Hope*. Paramus, NJ: Paulist Press, 1972.

Pinkola Estes, Clarissa. *The Faithful Gardner: A Wise Tale About That Which Can Never Die*. San Francisco: Harper, 1995.

Pinkola Estes, Ph.D., Clarissa. *Women Who Run with the Wolves: Myths and Stories of the Wild Woman Archetype*. New York: Ballantine Books, a division of Random House, Inc., 1992.

Scaer, M.D., Robert C.. *The Body Bears the Burden: Trauma, Dissociation, and Disease*. New York: Haworth Medical Press, 2001.

Siegel, M.D., Bernie S. *Peace, Love & Healing: Bodymind Communication & the Path to Self-Healing: An Exploration*. New York: Harper & Row, 1989.

Books for Younger Parts

Younger parts might enjoy these books (so might older parts!):

Bach, Richard. *Jonathan Livingston Seagull: A Story*. New York: Avon Books, a division of the Hearst Corporation, pub. by The Macmillan Company, 1973.

Brother Eagle, Sister Sky: the words of Chief Seattle/paintings by Susan Jeffers. New York: Dial Books, a division of Penguin Books USA, Inc., 1991.

Buscaglia, Leo F. *The Fall of Freddie the Leaf: A Story of Life for All Ages*. Thorofare: C.B. Slack; New York, N.Y.: Distributed by Holt, Rinehart and Winston, 1982.

Hanson, Warren. *The Next Place*. Minneapolis: Waldman House Press, 1997.

Howard, Jane R. , and Lynne Cherry (illus.). *When I'm Sleepy*. 1st ed. ed. New York: Dutton, 1985.

L'Engle, Madeleine. *A Wrinkle In Time*. New York: Scholastic Book Services, by arrangement with Farrar, Straus & Giroux, Inc., 1962.

Minogue, Frank , and Beth Lee Cripe (illus.). *Little Horse*. Golden Valley, MN: “Different” Books/The Place in the Woods, 2002.

Seuss, Dr. *Oh, The Places You'll Go*. New York: Random House, 1990.

Seuss, Dr. *Dr. Seuss's Sleep Book*. New York: Random House, 1990.

Silverstein, Shel. *The Missing Piece*. New York: HarperCollins, 1992.

Silverstein, Shel. *The Giving Tree*. 1st ed. New York: Harper & Row, 1976.

Williams, Margery , and David Jorgensen (illus.). *The Velveteen Rabbit*. 1st Dragonfly ed. ed. New York: Knopf : Distributed by Random House, 1990.

Websites

EMDR Institute provides more information about Eye Movement Desensitization and Reprocessing (EMDR), a technique which has helped many to overcome the aftermath of their traumatic experiences. They take into account the dissociative process (critical in order to not create more distress and upset and possibly set a dissociative person back), by requiring additional training for clinicians/therapists who wish to use this technique safely and effectively with persons with DID or other dissociative disorders.

http://www.emdr.com

Emotional Freedom Therapy—the technique commonly called 'tapping' has helped many find relief from anxiety and panic episodes, fears and phobias, and a wide variety of physical symptoms. A person can learn to use this technique themselves, and use its wide variety of applications to better assist themselves in overcoming many problems that hold them back from a better life.

http://www.emofree.com

Traumatic Incident Reduction Association, which offers more information about the trauma therapy technique called Traumatic Incident Reduction, which helps defuse the emotional charge of the trauma, gradually, over time, and in a unique, lasting, and highly effective way.

http://www.tir.org

This is the official US government Department of Justice Home Page website for the **Americans with Disabilities Act**. It includes many links that cover specific aspects of the ADA.

http://www.ada.gov

This site, affiliated with Boston University, is a good site for information about disabilities with relation to employment and schooling.

http://www.bu.edu/cpr/jobschool/sidebar.htm

Samaritans (as they call themselves), re a group operating (physically) in the United Kingdom/Great Britain, Ireland, and Wales, though the services they provide by email, postal mail and phone can be accessed by anyone, anywhere, no matter where they reside. It is a group run by lay-persons—professionally trained volunteers who aid those in crisis, or who are contemplating suicide, or who just need a kind and caring person to talk to. There is no charge, no obligation, and the service is completely anonymous and confidential.

http://www.samaritans.org

Survivorship is a non-profit organization that seeks to assist those whose trauma experience includes ritualized abuse (including Satanic Ritual Abuse), torture, and/or mind control. It is geared to help survivors, their supporters, and professionals who seek to help them. This is a good site, with helpful resources, information, and links, though a word of warning—some of what is there may be triggering to some.

http://www.Survivorship.org

Sidran Institute is a 'clearinghouse' type organization dedicated to providing education about trauma, trauma related matters, and dissociation. It has resources to assist survivors and their supporters, as well as professionals who work with those who have suffered and survived trauma. The site includes resources/ information about DID.

http://www.sidran.org

International Society for the Study of Dissociation, whose mission is to research and disseminate information about dissociation, and the diagnosis and treatment of dissociative disorders. This site also has some information about DID.

http://www.ISSD.org

Aiki Works, Incorporated was founded by Aikido Master Tom Crum. It has insightful and tested methods for stress reduction, conflict resolution, problem solving, better and more effective communication, and much else—all rooted in ideas whose genesis lies in the martial art of Aikido.

http://www.aikiworks.com

The last two sites are just "feel good" sites. They have beautiful music and graphics, and messages of affirmation and encouragement.

http://www.geocities.com/Heartland/Woods/7383/rainbows.html
http://www.geocities.com/Heartland/Woods/7383/purpose.html

Music

Enya. Paint the Sky with Stars: The Best of Enya. Reprise Records (CD), 1997.

Enya. A Day Without Rain. Reprise Records (CD), 2000.

Kitaro. The Best of Kitaro. Kuckuck records (CD), 1991.

Markoe, Gerald Jay. Celestial Mozart. Astro Music (CD), 1999.

Nakai, R. Carlos. Canyon Trilogy. Canyon Records (CD), 1992.

Noll, Shaina. Songs for the Inner Child. Singing Heart (CD), 1996.

Xumantra. Singing Bowls. First Light Music (CD), 1999.

Some find sound recordings of nature relaxing, others do not. Likewise, some find music with religious content reassuring, while others find it triggering or problematic. Each System needs to determine what is helpful and what is not.

Movies/Videos

The Dark Crystal. Dir. Jim Henson and Frank Oz. Buena Vista Home Video, 1994.

Dr Seuss' How the Grinch Stole Christmas/Horton Hears A Who. Warner Home Video, (1966, 2000).

The Fisher King. Dir. Terry Gilliam. Sony Pictures, 1991.

It's a Wonderful Life. Dir. Frank Capra. Liberty Films, 1946.

Appendix

A What's it Like To Be DID?

What's it Like To Share Your Self with Other Selves Inside?

It is often rather strange, interesting and fascinating, to say the least. It can infuse your life with unexpectedness and humor. It can also be unnerving, terrifying, and anxiety-producing until you become aware of the others and have learned how to co-exist within the body to a greater or lesser degree.

For example:

You may be the alter who falls asleep (or the part who awakens in the morning), but may not be the alter who has bad dreams or nightmares; the one who wakes up in the middle of the night may or may not be the one who had the nightmare.

Still other alters who did not have the nightmare or bad dream may have a nagging sense or feeling that resembles having dreamed, though they are (or may be), in reality picking up on dream images or dream feelings that were actually experienced by another part.

You may go out to eat and order, (or find you have ordered), more than one entree or beverage because different alters are hungry for different things—someone may order chicken, someone else may order medium rare roast beef, someone else a veggie burger, someone else a hotdog, or still another might order stir-fry. It might not be this extreme, but may have components of this type of menu; likewise with beverages: you may find a cup of coffee, a lemonade, a diet soda, and a glass of chocolate milk all sitting at your place setting.

This can look very strange in a restaurant, though it's easier to mask this if you are at a buffet or smorgasbord. At home, this scenario can still play out, but may not draw as much attention.

There may be food allergies as well as food preferences that are not shared or common to all parts.

For a lot of persons with DID, there are very often physiological changes or manifestations associated with switching between alters.

Some of these include headache, nausea, lightheadedness or disorientation, or visual disturbances. For some persons, the act of switching is tiring, or brings with it feelings of tiredness.

Being DID itself is often physically, mentally, and emotionally tiring.

Some Systems of alters report there being a 'hum of activity' inside all the time, as parts are talking amongst themselves, working on activities which comprise their own individual healing work, helping others inside who are having difficulties, working with young (sometimes very young) parts, and so on. If one is not accustomed to this (and sometimes even if one is), this 'hum' can be disorienting or distracting.

Some alters may be sleeping or resting while others are awake and engaged in activity.

There have been medical/scientific studies that have indicated different alters have different allergies (including drug allergies), different visual acuities, and a whole host (no pun intended) of various medical conditions or symptoms. Alters can have different EEG's, EKG's, different blood pressures, different blood glucose levels, different blood alcohol levels, different CAT and PET scans.

It is important for medical providers to know about the diagnosis of DID, and all that this diagnosis might entail. Otherwise, such conflicting data may baffle or hinder them assisting with the body's medical needs. There is even a chance of not being taken seriously and of genuine medical needs going un-addressed or untreated if the presentation appears too contradictory. For these same reasons, administering medications to persons with DID can be a challenging (occasionally potentially dangerous) proposition, and why psych meds are frequently ineffective.

Different alters will have different handwriting/writing styles. Some may be right handed while others are left handed while others are ambidextrous. A very young alter may not know how to write at all, and have to be (patiently) taught.

Alters can be of any age, from babies to the actual age of the body, while some claim an age even older. Alters can include male parts in a female body, or male parts in a female body. *

It is not uncommon for parts to see themselves (and see each other inside) as looking very different than the face or body that is reflected in a mirror. They may see themselves with a different face shape, or different color eyes, or hair of another color or style or length; they may see themselves as looking younger, thinner, or taller than a person looking at the physical body they reside in sees the body looking. A child alter may be frightened or distressed seeing a fifty-year-old body looking at him in the mirror; likewise a male alter may feel ashamed or challenged when he sees the girlish figure which stares back at him.

There may be parts who speak or write languages other parts do not know. There may be parts who speak with an accent, or drawl, or brogue, or who lisps, or stutters. It is possible to have parts who are functionally blind or deaf or who are learning disabled, dyslexic, or have other communication disorders.

Young parts may have difficulty with small motor skills or may have to count on their fingers, and may frequently misspell words.

It can be strange and wonderful (after you get used to it) for a stiff, sore, arthritic body to suddenly begin to skip, or get down on the floor to play 'trucks' or 'dinosaurs' or play with dolls, or color in a coloring book when a young part comes out to play.

Alter parts will likely have a wide variety of interests, experiences, skills and talents. There may be widely differing belief systems and orientations within a single System, from conservative to liberal; pious to skeptics to agnostics. Both a Baptist and Buddhist may inhabit one body. Likewise, it is possible to have a homosexual or bisexual alter when all the other alters are heterosexual. You may find vastly differing political opinions and ideologies in a System, as well. The System may need to come to some compromise/agreement if there is a desire to vote in an election, and have a designated part to go to the polls (and agree to vote as the System has agreed), so there is no possibility of embarrassment or of getting into trouble for 'trying to vote twice'.

For all these reasons, it is critical to get to know everyone who exists in one's System, and, unless parts are causing harm to the body or System, to figure out the ways and means of acceptance, tolerance, cooperation, and getting along. Just as in the outside world, you don't necessarily have to adopt someone's beliefs or lifestyle in order to respect them as a fellow human being and get along with them.

* Occasionally, there may even be non-human ('animal') parts.

Appendix

B Letters You Can Use

Many survivors of DID have difficulty making and keeping appointments with medical, dental, and other people in the helping professions. The following letters are examples you can use as-is or adapt to your special needs. Having it in writing helps guarantee your vulnerabilities are understood. It can also help you when there are several practitioners (nurse, intern, doctor) to whom you must communicate clearly with on a given office visit.

To Dr. ______________________, and whom it may concern,

I think it is important to let all new medical – health care providers know some things about me and my background. These are things that are very hard to say, but I think it is important you have more information about me so I can get the best care and treatment possible.

I have been badly abused. It has filled my life with fear and terror and doubt. I have a really, really hard time trusting anyone. Doctor visits and exams and procedures are very, very hard for me. Because of the trauma and abuse I suffered, I developed what is officially called Dissociative Identity Disorder (DID). This used to be called Multiple Personality Disorder. I am in therapy now, and working hard to heal from what was done to me.

It is really hard to stay 'present' and not dissociate when I/we feel scared. All of my alter parts have an agreement with each other and with our therapist that only one part will come to medical appointments. That seems like it would help to keep the fear and discomfort at a lower level. It would help me to stay present and focused and more calm if you were to call me by name from time to time—especially if I look like I'm 'spacing out' or getting frightened—and if you would tell me ahead of time before you are going to touch me or before you do anything, and explain beforehand what you are doing.

I hope you will be patient and know we are working hard to do something very difficult. In return we will always work to try to trust you and to be honest with you, and to cooperate in trying to take good care of our health.

If you have any concerns or questions, please call my therapist; that information is listed below. Thank you for your time and willingness to understand.

Sincerely,

Therapist name

Therapist address

Therapist phone

Therapist fax number

Therapist email address

To Dr. ______________________, and whom it may concern,

This letter is one which I write to all new health care providers to give them more information about my background.

I am a survivor of long term and extreme abuse and torture. I am in a safe situation now, and am in therapy with a skilled clinician who specializes in working with trauma survivors. My diagnosis is Dissociative Identity Disorder (DID—formerly Multiple Personality Disorder), and Post Traumatic Stress Disorder (PTSD). Both of these are a result of what was perpetrated against me—more rightly—against us.

We are growing stronger and healthier all the time, and the re-integration of alter personalities continues. There is one alter who attends all medical and health care appointments, as these are often difficult and stressful, frightening, and triggering for many parts. Having a designated part responsible for medical and health care appointments and exams and procedures has worked very well, and we anticipate no difficulties.

It is helpful to have things explained ahead of time, to have time to understand and integrate information, to be told ahead of time if there is touch, or whatever is involved in procedures, and so on. This lessens anxiety and stress.

If you have any concerns or questions regarding me/us, or about the diagnosis, or anything else, please feel free to contact my therapist, ____________________, at the address below. I am happy to sign a release of information form if needed.

Thank you for your time and sensitivity to this matter.

Sincerely,

Therapist name

Therapist address

Therapist phone

Therapist fax number

Therapist email address

Appendix

C About the Author

Just a note about the writer of this book...

We live in a female body, 44 years of age, single, a college graduate, with no living children. We share our life and living space with a beloved cat. We are beginning to work part-time, after being unable to work for over a decade. We were diagnosed DID in March 1997, though we had been in therapy intermittently, undiagnosed and misdiagnosed, for years.

We survived physical, sexual, emotional, and spiritual abuse and torture for the first 30 years of life, and intermittently for the next 9 years. The length of time, severity, and the extreme nature of what was done to us resulted in the creation of a very (very) large and diverse System. Perpetrators included family members, neighbors, school-mates—as well as the fathers of two school-mates, strangers, persons in authority in churches and schools we attended, and persons in the medical and mental health communities. We are also a survivor of SRA, and organized mind control programming by several different groups of individuals.

We self-mutilated for decades, attempted suicide several times, and ended up in a psych hospital once. We hated ourselves, we hated our life. We held no hope of anything ever changing, of the pain and horror and evil ever stopping. We didn't know life could be any different.

We finally found our way to a remarkable therapist, skilled both in treating trauma, and in accurately diagnosing DID and knowing what it takes to manage this diagnosis and re-integrate. We do not believe we would be here today without his skill, courage, compassion and unflagging belief in us, and his commitment to fight for us as long as we fought for ourselves.

Although we are not 100% in following what is in this book 100% of the time, we continue to work toward ever-higher levels of this, because the ideas contained in this book are what have saved us, and what gave us a real chance at a healthy, satisfying life. There is a lot of us in these pages.

Our successes have been hard-won, and they have not come quickly... but they have come.

Accepting the diagnosis, learning to accept each other inside and work together instead of trying to vex each other, learning through hard experience the critical importance of good self care, doing the wrenching work of remembering what was done to us and working through it—speaking our truth, feeling the feelings, doing the homework assignments... these are things that were incredibly, unbelievably difficult and time- and energy- consuming... difficult beyond what we believed we were capable of doing. Yet, standing where we are today, we say to you that it was worth it. And if sharing any of this helps you, it was worth it.

—atw
January 2005

Index

Q

R

S

Beyond Trauma:

Conversations on Traumatic Incident Reduction

"Not in 30+ years of practice have I used a more remarkably effective clinical procedure."
—Robert Moore, PhD

Victor Volkman (Ed.) takes the mystery out of one of the more remarkably effective clinical procedures in a way that can help millions of people revitalize and improve their lives. To those desperate people who have experienced trauma or tragedy, this process is a pathway to dealing with their feelings and getting on with their lives

In the new book **Beyond Trauma: Conversations on Traumatic Incident Reduction,** Volkman presents a series of conversations with a wide range of people from many different backgrounds and experiences. Each provides his or her perspective on Traumatic Incident Reduction, or TIR for short. The book explains the techniques used by professionals and patients to help people sort out, resolve and overcome the negative effects of painful suffering.

Readers will learn about how TIR has helped domestic violence survivors, crime victims, Vietnam vets, children, and others.

Praise *for Beyond Trauma*

"Beyond Trauma outlines the elements with clarity and insight as to how TIR will resolve wrestling with dilemmas, understanding your demons, and climbing out of emptiness."
—Sherry Russell, Grief Management Specialist and Author

"Our staff therapist is finding Beyond Trauma very helpful".
—Joan M. Renner, Director, Sexual Assault Program, YWCA of Clark County, WA

"Beyond Trauma is a recommended book for the professional or for the lay reader who wants to know about this technique before possibly seeking out a practitioner.
—Harold McFarland, Readers Preference Reviews

"Beyond Trauma: Conversations on Traumatic Incident Reduction is an excellent resource to begin one's mastery in this area of practice."
—Michael G. Tancyus, LCSW, DCSW, Augusta Behavioral Health

Loving Healing Press
Loving Healing Press
5145 Pontiac Trail
Ann Arbor, MI 48105
(734)662-6864
info@LovingHealing.com
Dist. Baker & Taylor

Pub. March 2004 — 316 pp trade/paper — 6"x9"
ISBN 1-932690-04-2 — $21.95 Retail

Includes appendices, biblio., resources, and index.
For general and academic libraries.

http:/www.BeyondTrauma.com

Lightning Source UK Ltd.
Milton Keynes UK
175364UK00004B/51/A
9 781932 690033